AF655009

REIMAGINING EDUCATION

A Global Vision for Inclusive and Innovative Learning

Based on the Book

The Future School

Dr. Subhash Nair

2025

Reimagining Education
A Global Vision for Inclusive and innovative Lear,ning

Subhash Nair

© 2025 Dr. Subhash Nair

Published by: Dr. Subhash Nair, Transform-Ed. First Edition: 2025

This book is based on The Future School by the same author, a visionary initiative to reimagine education through equity, innovation, and global collaboration. It is recommended for world leaders, educators, policymakers, and stakeholders committed to shaping the future of education, where transformation is not only inevitable but essential for the betterment of humanity and global well-being.

The content of this book reflects research, and vision of Dr. Subhash Nair, developed through extensive experience in educational transformation. Readers are encouraged to adapt the strategies to their specific contexts responsibly.

Transform-Ed is dedicated to fostering a global movement for educational equity and innovation. To learn more about the Global Future School Consortium and how to contribute to this transformative vision, visit https://biomees.com

CONTENTS

The Future School

A Blueprint for Global Educational Transformation

Welcome to the dawn of a new era in global education, envisioned by Dr. Subhash Nair's "The Future School." This infographics booklet distills the profound insights from 30 chapters into a vibrant, accessible guide for transforming learning worldwide. We believe education is not merely about imparting knowledge, but about nurturing human potential, fostering empathy, and building a sustainable, equitable future for all. This blueprint is a call to action for educators, policymakers, and communities to join the Global Future School Consortium (GFSC) and collectively redefine what's possible in learning.

The GFSC Vision: Uniting for a Brighter Future

The Global Future School Consortium (GFSC) is a visionary initiative designed to reimagine education through equity, innovation, and global collaboration. It's a worldwide network committed to transforming schools into dynamic hubs where every student feels seen, every idea is celebrated, and every lesson prepares young minds to shape a better world. Through shared open-source resources, collaborative policies, and a collective commitment, the GFSC ensures that transformative opportunities are accessible to every learner, regardless of their background, ability, or location.

Our Core Principles

- **Equity & Inclusion:** Ensuring every learner has access to quality education tailored to their unique needs.
- **Innovation & Adaptability:** Embracing new pedagogies and technologies to foster creativity and critical thinking.

- **Global Collaboration:** Connecting classrooms and communities worldwide to solve real-world problems.
- **Holistic Well-being:** Prioritizing mental, emotional, and social health alongside academic growth.
- **Sustainability:** Empowering students to become stewards of our planet and advocates for environmental justice.

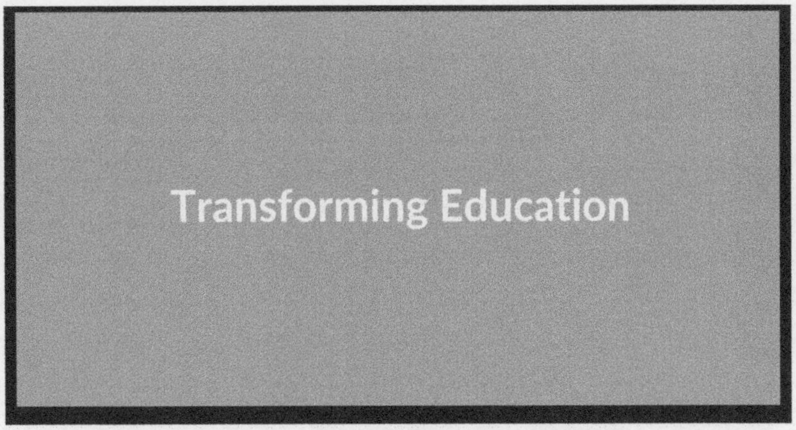

A Call to Action: Join the Transformation

The transformation of education is not merely inevitable, but essential for the betterment of humanity and global well-being. This booklet provides the practical steps and visionary insights needed to embark on this journey. We invite you to be an active participant in shaping this future.

How You Can Contribute

- **For Educators:** Embrace student-centered models, integrate interdisciplinary projects, and leverage open-source tools. Utilize GFSC lesson plans and professional development webinars to refine your practice and foster a growth mindset in your students.
- **For Policymakers:** Advocate for flexible curriculum standards, invest in accessible technology, and support policies that prioritize mental health and equity. Champion the GFSC framework to scale innovative practices across your regions.
- **For Community Leaders:** Partner with local schools to create civic and cultural hubs. Offer real-world project prompts, mentorship, and resources. Engage families in school decision-making and celebrate diverse cultural heritage.
- **For Parents & Stakeholders:** Actively participate in school vision committees, attend workshops, and provide feedback. Support initiatives that promote personalized learning, digital literacy, and social-emotional well-being for your children.

The Path Forward: Collective Impact

By uniting under the GFSC, we can create a powerful, synergistic movement. Imagine:

- **Global Resource Sharing:** A free digital repository of vision templates, case studies, and multilingual resources accessible to every school.
- **Collaborative Innovation:** Teachers and students worldwide co-creating solutions for global challenges, from climate change to social justice.
- **Equitable Access:** Ensuring every learner, regardless of their circumstances, has access to transformative educational opportunities.

This is our shared canvas, inviting every nation, every community, and every individual to craft the future school of innovation—a promise of a better world. Let's build it together.

Chapter 1 Vision

1. Envisioning The Future School: A Blueprint For Transformation

Key Ideas: Redefining Education

The future school is a dynamic, inclusive institution that prioritizes student agency, equity, and global awareness, redefining education as a lifelong, holistic journey.

- **Shift to Student-Centred Models:** Moving away from one-size-fits-all education to flexible approaches tailored to individual needs. For example, allowing students to choose project topics or offering varied instructional formats like hands-on activities and digital platforms.
- **Emphasize Creativity, Critical Thinking, and Collaboration:** These are the core pillars, replacing rote memorization. Students design eco-friendly projects, analyze sustainable energy options, and work with global peers on shared challenges.
- **Schools as Hubs for Community, Innovation, and Global Connection:** Schools transcend traditional boundaries, hosting cultural fairs, nurturing student-led apps for local needs, and linking students worldwide through virtual exchanges on platforms like ePals.

Actionable Strategies: Making Transformation Practical

- **Form a School Vision Committee:** Organize annual events where stakeholders brainstorm ways to personalize education (e.g., flexible schedules, adaptive tech). Use GFSC guides to structure sessions. *Timeline: Quarterly events, ongoing.*

- **Integrate 21st-Century Skills:** Include creativity, critical thinking, and collaboration in the mission statement. Commit to weekly group projects using GFSC rubrics. *Metric: 20% increase in student-led projects within 6 months.*
- **Become a Community Hub:** Craft a mission statement committing to quarterly community events and global projects. Plan a "Global Innovation Day" shared virtually with GFSC partner schools. *Timeline: Quarterly events, 1-year goal.*
- **Pilot a "Future School Lab":** Test student-centered methods in one grade level (e.g., 7th grade) before scaling up. Introduce a flipped classroom model using free Khan Academy resources. *Metric: 15% increase in student engagement in pilot within 3 months.*

This chapter lays the foundation for a revolutionary educational model, envisioning schools as dynamic hubs for personalized, inclusive, and innovative learning, moving beyond traditional, rigid systems. Dr. Nair introduces the Global Future School Consortium (GFSSC) to unite stakeholders in promoting inclusivity, affordability, and global connectivity. The vision reimagines schools as community centers fostering creativity, critical thinking, and social progress. Key strategies include forming school vision committees to brainstorm personalized learning approaches, integrating one personalized element per semester (e.g., goal-setting sessions), and leveraging subsidized internet access to connect low-resource schools globally. The chapter emphasizes actionable steps like annual stakeholder events and data collection to scale successful practices. It highlights the broader impact of transforming education into a force for human well-being, addressing disparities and fostering compassionate, interconnected societies. A specimen lesson plan encourages students to co-create their ideal school vision, aligning with GFSSC principles. The chapter sets a bold tone, advocating for a shift from one-size-fits-all education to flexible, student-centered models that empower learners to thrive in a rapidly changing world. By establishing a GFSSC charter, the vision ensures inclusivity and affordability, making transformative education accessible worldwide. The ultimate goal is to create schools that are engines of social and global progress, uplifting humanity through innovation and equity.

Broader Impact on Humanity and Well-Being

These key ideas collectively transform education into a force for human progress by prioritizing equity, creativity, and connection. Student-centered models ensure every learner has access to education that respects their individuality, reducing disparities. Emphasizing creativity, critical thinking, and collaboration equips students to innovate solutions for global challenges like climate change. Positioning schools as hubs strengthens community resilience and builds global understanding, fostering a civilization rooted in caring and mutual support.

Policy Highlight

Establish a Global Future School Consortium (GFSC) to collaboratively define and promote a shared vision for transformative education.

- Create a GFSC charter outlining principles of inclusivity, innovation, and affordability, accessible to all member schools.
- Require member schools to form local vision committees with students, educators, parents, and community leaders to align with GFSC goals.
- Share vision statements via an open-access GFSC platform to inspire global adoption.

Implementation Plan (12 months):

- **Q2 Year 1:** Launch GFSC, invite schools via global networks (e.g., UNESCO ASPnet), create online portal for sign-ups.
- **Q3 Year 1:** Host virtual global summit to draft GFSC charter (e.g., Zoom with live translation).
- **Q4 Year 1:** Require member schools to form local vision committees; provide free GFSC toolkit (agendas, templates).
- **Q1 Year 2:** Launch open-access GFSC platform to share vision statements and case studies (e.g., GitHub Pages).

Resource Sharing: Use Google Drive for free templates. **Inclusivity:** Multilingual templates, virtual participation, subsidized internet access via NGOs.

Specimen Lesson Plan

Lesson: Co-creating Our Future School Vision

Objective: Students co-create a vision for their ideal school, aligning with the Global Future School Consortium (GFSC) charter.
Grade Level: 6–12
Materials: Whiteboard, markers, GFSC vision template (from GFSC platform), access to Google Docs.

Activities:

- (10 min) Discuss: What makes a school inspiring? Use GFSC charter principles (shared on platform).
- (20 min) Small groups: Brainstorm ideas for a student-centered school vision using the GFSC template.
- (20 min) Groups present ideas; class votes on key elements to include in a shared vision statement.
- (10 min) Reflection: Students write a short paragraph on how their vision supports inclusivity.

Assessment: Evaluate group visions for creativity and alignment with GFSC principles; collect reflections.
Inclusivity: Provide translated templates; allow verbal or drawn responses for diverse learners.

Chapter 2 Learning Spaces

2. Redesigning Learning Spaces: Flexible And Accessible Environments

Key Ideas: Transforming Classrooms

Redesigning learning spaces into flexible, accessible environments revolutionizes global education by fostering creativity and collaboration, breaking down physical and digital barriers.

- **Modular Classrooms:** Movable furniture for group work, individual study, or presentations. Tables can be clustered for brainstorming or spread out for quiet reading, fostering student agency and accommodating diverse learning styles.
- **Virtual Reality (VR) and Augmented Reality (AR) Spaces:** Immersive learning experiences that transport students beyond the classroom, like virtual field trips to ancient ruins or interactive biology simulations. Uses affordable, smartphone-compatible headsets.
- **Outdoor Learning Areas:** Connecting students with nature, fostering environmental awareness and well-being. Simple setups with benches, shade, and Wi-Fi enable lessons in fresh air, like science experiments in school gardens.

Actionable Strategies: Building Flexible Environments

- **Replace Fixed Desks with Modular Furniture:** Transition to wheeled tables and stackable chairs, using GFSC blueprints to source or build furniture from local materials. *Cost: ~$500 per classroom. Timeline: Pilot in 1 classroom within 3 months.*

- **Create a Low-Cost VR Corner:** Set up a VR corner using affordable headsets (e.g., Google Cardboard, ~$10 each) and free apps like Google Expeditions. *Cost: ~$50 for 5 headsets. Timeline: Pilot in 1 classroom within 3 months.*
- **Partner with Local Parks for Outdoor Classrooms:** Collaborate with nearby parks or community spaces to develop outdoor classrooms, installing weatherproof seating and portable Wi-Fi hotspots. *Cost: ~$200 for seating. Timeline: Weekly lessons within 6 months.*
- **Involve Students in Design:** Host a "Classroom Redesign Challenge" where students propose furniture layouts, fostering ownership and creativity. Winning designs can be implemented with GFSC guides. *Metric: 25% increase in student satisfaction with learning spaces within 1 year.*

This chapter reimagines learning spaces as dynamic, inclusive environments that break from traditional classroom designs. It advocates for flexible, modular spaces with movable walls, digital tools for rural connectivity, and outdoor areas to foster environmental consciousness. The goal is to create affordable, accessible spaces that promote collaboration and inclusivity. Strategies include hosting “Classroom Redesign Challenges” where students propose layouts, using low-cost furniture like stackable chairs, and mandating flexible designs through the GFSSC network. Outdoor learning areas, equipped with Wi-Fi and weatherproof seating, connect students with nature, enhancing mental health and climate awareness. The chapter emphasizes pragmatic implementation, such as rotating activities weekly to maximize space and using colorful tape to mark collaborative zones. A specimen lesson plan encourages students to co-create their ideal learning environment, aligning with GFSSC goals. The approach bridges geographical and economic gaps, ensuring even low-resource schools can adopt these changes. By fostering ownership through student involvement and leveraging GFSSC’s shared resources, the chapter envisions schools as hubs for community engagement and global understanding. The broader impact is creating learning spaces that nurture creativity, empathy, and environmental stewardship, equipping students to tackle global challenges like climate change while promoting equitable access to quality education.

Broader Impact on Humanity and Well-Being

These key ideas transform education by creating flexible, immersive, and nature-connected learning environments. Modular classrooms empower diverse learners, fostering collaboration and creativity. VR/AR spaces make education exciting and accessible, bridging geographical and economic gaps. Outdoor learning areas nurture environmental consciousness and mental health, equipping students to tackle climate challenges and live healthier lives.

Policy Highlight

Mandate flexible, low-cost learning space designs shared through the GFSC network.

- Develop open-source blueprints for modular classrooms and outdoor learning areas.
- Encourage schools to adapt designs using local materials to reduce costs.
- Provide GFSC-funded training on integrating virtual learning platforms.

Implementation Plan (10 months):

- **Q2 Year 2:** Form GFSC design task force to create open-source blueprints (e.g., SketchUp).
- **Q3 Year 2:** Pilot designs in 10 diverse schools (urban, rural, low-resource) via GFSC grants.
- **Q4 Year 2:** Share blueprints and virtual tour videos on GFSC platform, encourage local adaptations.
- **Q1 Year 3:** Train teachers via webinars on integrating virtual platforms (e.g., Moodle).

Resource Sharing: 3D models and virtual tour videos on GFSC platform. **Inclusivity:** Designs accessible for students with disabilities, offline blueprints.

Specimen Lesson Plan

Lesson: Designing Our Ideal Learning Space

Objective: Students co-create a vision for their ideal school's learning spaces, aligning with flexible and accessible principles.
Grade Level: 6–12
Materials: Whiteboard, markers, GFSC space design templates, recycled materials, access to Google Docs.

Activities:

- (10 min) Discuss: What makes an inspiring learning space? Use GFSC design principles.
- (20 min) Small groups: Brainstorm ideas for flexible classroom layouts or outdoor learning areas using GFSC templates.
- (20 min) Groups present ideas; class votes on key elements to include in a shared design vision, potentially building a small model from recycled materials.
- (10 min) Reflection: Students write a short paragraph on how their design supports inclusivity and collaboration.

Assessment: Evaluate group designs for creativity, feasibility, and alignment with GFSC principles; collect reflections.
Inclusivity: Provide translated templates; allow verbal or drawn responses for diverse learners.

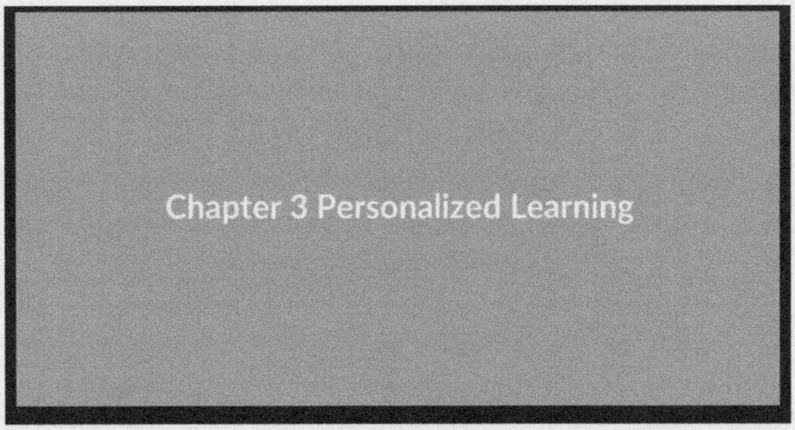

3. Personalised Learning: Tailoring Education to Every Student

Key Ideas: Education for Every Individual

Personalized learning, powered by open-source adaptive platforms, transforms global education by ensuring every student's unique needs and pace are met.

- **Adaptive Learning Platforms:** Dynamically adjust content difficulty based on student performance. Platforms like Khan Academy offer tailored paths in subjects like math or reading, providing immediate feedback.
- **Student-Led Goal-Setting:** Empowering students to set their own learning goals, aligning education with their passions. Students reflect on strengths, set achievable goals, and track progress with teacher support.
- **Flexible Pathways:** Allow students to progress at their own pace, accessing advanced content or remedial support as needed. Uses digital platforms, project-based options, and teacher guidance to create individualized tracks.

Actionable Strategies: Implementing Personalization

- **Implement Free Adaptive Platforms:** Adopt platforms like Khan Academy or Google Classroom for individualized assignments. Integrate into weekly math exercises. *Cost: ~$200 for a classroom computer. Timeline: Pilot in 1 subject within 3 months.*

- **Schedule Weekly Student-Teacher Check-Ins:** Allocate 10-15 minutes weekly for one-on-one or small-group check-ins to set and review personalized goals using GFSC templates. *Timeline: Weekly, ongoing.*
- **Offer "Passion Project" Periods:** Dedicate one hour weekly to self-directed topics with teacher guidance, using GFSC project templates. Students research renewable energy or practice algebra. *Timeline: Weekly, ongoing.*
- **Create Learning Menus:** Use GFSC templates to design "menus" of advanced and remedial activities for each unit, allowing students to choose tasks matching their level. *Metric: 15% higher engagement in personalized programs.*

This chapter champions personalized learning, tailoring education to individual student strengths, interests, and learning paces to enhance engagement and outcomes. It advocates for adaptive learning platforms like Khan Academy and Google Classroom, which adjust content difficulty based on performance, ensuring inclusivity for diverse learners. Key strategies include implementing open-source adaptive platforms across GFSSC schools, offering “passion project” periods for self-directed learning, and using digital tools to create individualized tracks. Student-led goal-setting empowers learners to align education with personal interests, supported by teacher guidance and offline resources for low-tech settings. A specimen lesson plan guides students to set personal goals using adaptive platforms, fostering autonomy. The chapter emphasizes affordability and scalability, making personalized learning accessible globally, particularly in resource-constrained areas. By breaking from traditional, uniform curricula, it aims to improve academic outcomes and engagement, especially for underserved students. The broader impact is an education system that uplifts humanity by addressing diverse needs, reducing dropout rates, and fostering lifelong learning. The GFSSC’s role ensures equitable access through free platforms and multilingual resources, creating a compassionate, interconnected world where every student thrives.

Broader Impact on Humanity and Well-Being

These key ideas transform education by making it deeply personal, inclusive, and empowering. Adaptive platforms ensure equitable access, closing achievement gaps and fostering confidence. Student-led goal-setting builds agency and resilience, preparing students to contribute creatively. Flexible pathways accommodate all learners, promoting fairness and curiosity, equipping students to address global challenges.

Policy Highlight

Implement open-source adaptive learning platforms across GFSC schools.

- Adopt free platforms like Khan Academy or Moodle for personalized curricula.
- Require teacher training on adaptive tools, offered via GFSC webinars.
- Set guidelines for student-led goal-setting sessions twice per term.

Implementation Plan (9 months):

- **Q2 Year 2:** Select free platforms (e.g., Khan Academy, Moodle), test compatibility in 5 pilot schools.
- **Q3 Year 2:** Train teachers via GFSC webinars on platform use and goal-setting strategies.
- **Q4 Year 2:** Implement weekly student-teacher check-ins for goal-setting, using GFSC templates.
- **Q1 Year 1:** Scale platforms to all GFSC schools, with offline content options for low-connectivity areas.

Resource Sharing: GFSC database of adaptive tools and tutorials. **Inclusivity:** Multilingual platforms, offline access (USB-based content).

Specimen Lesson Plan

Lesson: Setting Personal Learning Goals with Adaptive Platforms

Objective: Students set personal learning goals using adaptive platforms.
Grade Level: 4–12
Materials: Khan Academy accounts, GFSC goal-setting template, notebooks.

Activities:

- (10 min) Demo Khan Academy; explain how it adapts to individual pace.
- (20 min) Students explore Khan Academy, select one topic, and set a learning goal using the GFSC template.
- (20 min) Pair discussion: Share goals and how they align with personal interests.
- (10 min) Reflection: Students write about how personalized learning feels empowering.

Assessment: Review goals for specificity; assess reflections for engagement.
Inclusivity: Provide offline goal templates; support multilingual platform access.

Chapter 4 AI in Education

4. The Role of AI in Education: Enhancing Teaching and Learning

Key Ideas: AI as an Ethical Tool

Ethical AI integration revolutionizes global education by automating routine tasks and personalizing instruction, freeing teachers to focus on creativity and human connection.

- **AI-Driven Tutoring Systems:** Provide instant, personalized support for homework or challenging concepts (e.g., Duolingo for language, Socratic for math). Available 24/7, ensuring accessibility for all students.
- **Automated Grading:** AI evaluates objective assessments (e.g., multiple-choice tests), instantly scoring responses and providing feedback. This frees teachers for creative instruction and personalized support.
- **AI Analytics:** Provide teachers with actionable insights into student performance, identifying strengths and areas for improvement. Enables targeted interventions without extensive manual analysis.

Actionable Strategies: Integrating AI Ethically

- **Use AI Tools like Duolingo or Socratic:** Implement GFSC-recommended tools for language practice or math problem-solving. Integrate into weekly assignments. *Cost: ~$100 for shared tablet. Timeline: Pilot in 1 subject within 3 months.*
- **Train Teachers on AI Dashboards:** Equip teachers with GFSC-vetted tools (e.g., Moodle, Google Forms with AI plugins) to track student progress securely. *Timeline:*

2-hour webinar training, ongoing.

- **Pilot AI Chatbots for After-Hours Support:** Deploy GFSC-approved AI chatbots (e.g., open-source Dialogflow) for homework help, programmed with vetted resources. *Cost: Minimal. Timeline: Pilot in 1 grade within 6 months.*
- **Integrate AI Ethics Discussions:** Include debates on social media privacy or algorithmic bias in tech classes, using GFSC case studies. *Metric: 12% improvement in learning outcomes with personalized AI instruction.*

This chapter explores the ethical integration of artificial intelligence (AI) to enhance teaching and learning while prioritizing human values. AI is envisioned as a supportive tool, not a replacement for teachers, offering personalized tutoring and analytics to identify student strengths and gaps. Key strategies include creating AI tutoring schedules (e.g., one hour weekly), developing open-source question banks to reduce teacher workload, and sharing simplified analytics with students and parents via GFSSC formats. Offline apps ensure accessibility in low-connectivity areas, making AI inclusive for rural schools. A specimen lesson plan involves students exploring ethical AI use through simulated tutoring sessions, fostering critical thinking. The chapter emphasizes privacy and affordability, using GFSSC guides to ensure ethical implementation. By aligning with 2025's technological trends, AI-driven tools enhance efficiency and equity in education. The broader impact is a transformative system where AI supports personalized learning, reduces teacher burnout, and bridges educational gaps globally. The GFSSC's role in providing low-bandwidth solutions and ethical guidelines ensures that AI uplifts diverse learners, fostering a compassionate, innovative educational landscape that prepares students for a tech-driven future.

Broader Impact on Humanity and Well-Being

These key ideas transform education by leveraging AI to make learning personalized, efficient, and inclusive. AI tutoring provides equitable access to support, boosting confidence. Automated grading frees teachers for creative instruction, fostering critical thinking. AI analytics enable precise interventions, ensuring no student is left behind, promoting equity and preparing learners for global challenges.

Policy Highlight

Promote ethical AI integration with GFSC-developed guidelines.

- Deploy open-source AI tools for tutoring and grading, vetted by GFSC for privacy compliance.
- Mandate annual teacher training on AI ethics and data security.
- Create a GFSC AI hub to share tools like chatbots or analytics dashboards.

Implementation Plan (10 months):

- **Q2 Year 2:** Develop GFSC AI ethics guidelines with global educator input.
- **Q3 Year 2:** Deploy open-source AI tools (e.g., tutoring chatbots, grading systems) in 10 pilot schools.
- **Q4 Year 2:** Train teachers via GFSC webinars on AI ethics and data privacy.
- **Q1 Year 3:** Create a GFSC AI hub for tool sharing and troubleshooting.

Resource Sharing: Free AI toolkits and implementation guides on GFSC platform. **Inclusivity:** Multilingual AI tools, accessible on low-cost devices.

Specimen Lesson Plan

Lesson: Exploring Ethical AI in Education

Objective: Students explore ethical AI use through a simulated tutoring session.
Grade Level: 7–12
Materials: GFSC AI ethics guidelines, access to an open-source AI chatbot (e.g., Dialogflow), paper.

Activities:

- (10 min) Discuss GFSC AI ethics guidelines; focus on privacy and fairness.
- (20 min) Pairs: Use a GFSC-approved AI chatbot to solve a math or language problem.
- (20 min) Class debate: Benefits vs. risks of AI in education.
- (10 min) Reflection: Students write about responsible AI use.

Assessment: Evaluate debate participation and reflection depth.
Inclusivity: Provide text-based AI interfaces for accessibility; translate guidelines.

Chapter 5 PBL

5. Project-Based Learning: Real-World Problem Solving as Core Curriculum

Key Ideas: Learning by Doing

Project-based learning transforms global education by embedding real-world problem-solving into curricula, fostering critical thinking and collaboration.

- **Projects Tied to Local or Global Issues:** Students design solutions for challenges like sustainable community gardens or global reforestation campaigns. Integrates math, science, and social studies.
- **Collaborative Teams:** Students take on roles (e.g., project manager, researcher) to mimic workplace dynamics. Teaches teamwork, communication, and conflict resolution.
- **Public Showcases:** Students present solutions to authentic audiences (parents, community, global peers) through fairs or presentations. Builds confidence, communication skills, and civic engagement.

Actionable Strategies: Implementing PBL

- **Partner with Local Businesses:** Collaborate with local organizations (e.g., farms, recycling centers) to provide real-world project prompts. *Timeline: One partnership meeting, ongoing projects.*

- **Dedicate One Day per Week to PBL:** Reserve one school day (e.g., Fridays) for PBL, blending subjects like math, science, and communication. *Timeline: Weekly, ongoing.*
- **Host a Quarterly "Solution Fair":** Organize fairs where students display projects (e.g., recycling campaigns) via posters, videos, or live demos. *Cost: ~$50 for materials. Timeline: Quarterly.*
- **Connect with Global Teams:** Pair local teams with GFSC partner schools for virtual collaboration on shared projects (e.g., global recycling initiative) using platforms like ePals. *Metric: 20% increase in student engagement.*

This chapter positions project-based learning (PBL) as the cornerstone of education, focusing on real-world problem-solving and competency-based evaluation. It proposes dedicating 20% of instructional time to PBL, using GFSSC's open-source project library to design tasks like sustainable community solutions. Strategies include hosting project showcases for authentic audiences, establishing partnerships with local organizations, and involving media to highlight student work. A specimen lesson plan guides students to design community-based projects, fostering collaboration and critical thinking. The approach redefines success beyond test scores, emphasizing skills like teamwork and innovation. By leveraging GFSSC's virtual platforms for global input, PBL becomes inclusive and scalable, even in low-resource settings with minimal technology. The chapter aligns with 2025's emphasis on practical skills, preparing students for careers in fields like green technology. The broader impact is an education system that equips students to address global challenges, fostering resilience and social responsibility. The GFSSC ensures accessibility through free resources and offline guides, creating a compassionate, interconnected world where students thrive as proactive problem-solvers.

Broader Impact on Humanity and Well-Being

These key ideas transform education by making it relevant, collaborative, and impactful. Projects tied to real issues foster environmental and social responsibility. Collaborative teams build teamwork and empathy, preparing students for cooperative careers. Public showcases instill confidence and civic engagement, strengthening community bonds.

Policy Highlight

Require all GFSC schools to dedicate 20% of instructional time to project-based learning (PBL).

- Develop a GFSC PBL framework with templates for interdisciplinary projects.
- Partner with global NGOs to provide real-world project prompts (e.g., water conservation).
- Host virtual "Solution Fairs" to showcase student projects globally.

Implementation Plan (9 months):

- **Q2 Year 2:** Develop GFSC PBL framework with templates.
- **Q3 Year 2:** Partner with NGOs (e.g., WaterAid) for project prompts; pilot in 10 schools.
- **Q4 Year 2:** Train teachers on PBL facilitation via GFSC webinars.
- **Q1 Year 3:** Host virtual "Solution Fairs" on Zoom, showcasing student projects globally.

Resource Sharing: PBL lesson plans and rubrics on GFSC platform. **Inclusivity:** Projects addressing local community needs, translated for diverse contexts.

Specimen Lesson Plan

Lesson: Designing a Community-Based Project

Objective: Students design a community-based project to address a local issue.
Grade Level: 6–12
Materials: GFSC PBL template, local issue list (e.g., recycling), poster paper.

Activities:

- (10 min) Introduce GFSC PBL framework; discuss a local issue (e.g., waste management).
- (25 min) Small groups: Plan a project using the GFSC template (e.g., a school recycling campaign).
- (15 min) Groups present project outlines to class.
- (10 min) Reflection: Students write about how their project benefits the community.

Assessment: Evaluate project plans for feasibility and creativity; review reflections.
Inclusivity: Include local issues relevant to diverse student backgrounds; allow multilingual presentations.

Chapter 6 SEL

6. Social-Emotional Learning: Nurturing Empathy and Resilience

Key Ideas: Nurturing the Whole Child

Focuses on embedding SEL into the curriculum to develop emotional intelligence, self-awareness, and interpersonal skills, fostering resilient, inclusive communities.

- **Daily Mindfulness Exercises:** Brief, 5-minute activities (e.g., deep breathing, guided meditations) to reduce anxiety and improve focus. GFSC provides free, multilingual scripts and audio files.
- **Peer Support Circles:** Structured, weekly discussions where students share challenges, feelings, or ideas in a safe, respectful environment. Fosters trust, reduces isolation, and teaches diverse perspectives.
- **SEL Integrated into Academic Subjects:** Weaving emotional and social skills within existing lessons. For example, analyzing characters' emotions in literature or reflecting on teamwork in science experiments.

Actionable Strategies: Fostering Empathy and Resilience

- **Start Classes with 5-Minute Mindfulness:** Implement GFSC-curated mindfulness exercises using free apps like Calm or Headspace, or GFSC's offline audio scripts. *Cost: Minimal. Timeline: Daily, ongoing.*

- **Train Students to Lead "Empathy Circles":** Use GFSC circle guides to train student facilitators to lead weekly 15-minute empathy circles. *Timeline: Weekly, ongoing.*
- **Incorporate SEL Themes into Existing Lessons:** Use GFSC lesson plans to embed SEL in subjects, such as discussing characters' emotions in literature or collaboration in science labs. *Timeline: Weekly, ongoing.*
- **Create Mindfulness Corners:** Designate a quiet classroom corner with GFSC-provided posters and cushions for independent practice. *Metric: 30% drop in behavioral issues.*

This chapter underscores the importance of social-emotional learning (SEL) to foster empathy, resilience, and supportive school environments. It proposes integrating daily mindfulness exercises, peer support circles, and SEL into academic subjects like literature and history to enhance emotional intelligence. Strategies include dedicating 20% of instructional time to SEL, using offline scripts for low-resource schools, and training teachers via GFSSC webinars. A specimen lesson plan encourages students to design community projects addressing local issues, reinforcing empathy. The approach reduces anxiety, improves focus, and promotes social cohesion, particularly for diverse learners. By embedding SEL in curricula, schools create inclusive environments that support mental health and conflict resolution. The chapter aligns with 2025's focus on post-COVID mental health needs, ensuring accessibility through free resources. The broader impact is a global education system that nurtures compassionate, resilient students equipped to handle life's challenges. The GFSSC's role in providing multilingual, offline materials ensures equity, fostering harmonious communities worldwide through empathy-driven education.

Broader Impact on Humanity and Well-Being

These key ideas transform education by prioritizing emotional and social development, creating inclusive, supportive environments. Daily mindfulness reduces stress and improves focus. Peer support circles build empathy and communication, reducing conflict. SEL integration ensures emotional intelligence is a universal skill, preparing students to address global challenges with compassion.

Policy Highlight

Mandate social-emotional learning (SEL) integration in GFSC schools.

- Implement daily mindfulness exercises and peer support circles.
- Integrate SEL into academic subjects using GFSC lesson plans.
- Provide GFSC training for teachers on SEL facilitation.

Implementation Plan (9 months):

- **Q2 Year 2:** Develop GFSC SEL framework with lesson plans.
- **Q3 Year 2:** Pilot mindfulness exercises and peer circles in 10 schools.
- **Q4 Year 2:** Train teachers via GFSC webinars on SEL integration.
- **Q1 Year 3:** Scale to all GFSC schools, with multilingual resources.

Resource Sharing: SEL lesson plans and guides on GFSC platform. **Inclusivity:** Multilingual resources, offline activities.

Specimen Lesson Plan

Lesson: Practicing Mindfulness for Stress Management

Objective: Students practice a mindfulness technique to manage stress.
Grade Level: 3–12
Materials: GFSC mindfulness guide, quiet space, optional Calm app access.

Activities:

- (10 min) Introduce mindfulness using GFSC guide; model deep breathing.
- (20 min) Practice a 5-minute guided mindfulness exercise.
- (20 min) Discuss: How did it feel? Share stress management tips.
- (10 min) Reflection: Students write about how mindfulness can help daily life.

Assessment: Observe participation; evaluate reflections.
Inclusivity: Offer non-verbal reflection options; translate guides.

Chapter 7 Global Citizenship

7. Global Citizenship: Preparing Students for a Connected World

Key Ideas: Cultivating Global Perspectives

Fostering global citizenship through virtual exchanges and shared curricula transforms education by preparing students to collaborate across cultures.

- **Virtual Exchange Programs:** Connect students with peers in other countries through digital platforms (e.g., PenPal Schools) for collaborative projects and cultural exchanges. Fosters cross-cultural understanding.
- **Curricula Focused on Global Issues:** Embedding topics like climate change, human rights, or gender equality into curricula. Uses interdisciplinary approaches to foster critical thinking and civic engagement.
- **Language Learning Emphasizing Cultural Context:** Goes beyond grammar, exploring cultural traditions and histories alongside language acquisition. Builds intercultural competence for respectful communication.

Actionable Strategies: Connecting Classrooms Worldwide

- **Partner with Platforms like PenPal Schools:** Connect classrooms for semester-long projects, such as creating a joint digital magazine on sustainability. *Cost: Minimal. Timeline: Pilot in 1 classroom within 3 months.*
- **Integrate UN Sustainable Development Goals (SDGs):** Incorporate GFSC-provided SDG lesson plans into science and social studies. Students design solar ovens or role-

play equality debates. *Timeline: Weekly lessons, ongoing.*

- **Offer Free Language Apps alongside Cultural Workshops:** Implement Duolingo for weekly language practice, supplemented by monthly cultural workshops led by community volunteers. *Cost: Minimal. Timeline: Ongoing.*
- **Host Virtual Cultural Fairs:** Organize quarterly events where students present cultural traditions to partner schools via Zoom. *Metric: 20% increase in cross-cultural understanding.*

This chapter focuses on preparing students to address global issues like climate change and human rights through cross-cultural collaboration. It advocates for curricula emphasizing global challenges, virtual exchanges via GFSSC platforms like PenPal Schools, and language learning with cultural context to foster empathy. Strategies include mandating global exchange programs, hosting cultural workshops with community volunteers, and creating digital galleries of student work. A specimen lesson plan involves students collaborating with global peers on shared issues, promoting cultural competence. The chapter aligns with 2025's sustainability and peace goals, ensuring inclusivity through offline exchange options. By connecting classrooms worldwide, it bridges cultural divides and encourages proactive citizenship. The broader impact is a compassionate, interconnected world where students drive sustainable progress. The GFSSC's role in facilitating virtual platforms and low-cost resources ensures accessibility, empowering students globally to become empathetic, responsible global citizens who tackle pressing challenges with mutual respect and collaboration.

Broader Impact on Humanity and Well-Being

These key ideas transform education by fostering global citizenship. Virtual exchanges build cross-cultural understanding and promote peace. Curricula on global issues inspire action on climate change and human rights. Language learning with cultural context enhances mutual respect, breaking down barriers and fostering inclusive communities.

Policy Highlight

Require GFSC schools to participate in global exchange programs.

- Facilitate virtual exchanges via GFSC partnerships with platforms like ePals.
- Integrate UN Sustainable Development Goals into curricula.
- Offer multilingual resources for global issue discussions.

Implementation Plan (10 months):

- **Q2 Year 2:** Partner with platforms like ePals for virtual exchanges.
- **Q3 Year 2:** Develop curricula on UN Sustainable Development Goals, shared freely via GFSC.
- **Q4 Year 2:** Pilot exchanges in 10 schools, with feedback shared globally.
- **Q1 Year 3:** Scale exchanges to all GFSC schools, with GFSC subsidies for internet access.

Resource Sharing: Exchange templates and curricula on GFSC platform. **Inclusivity:** Multilingual resources, offline exchange options (e.g., letter-writing).

Specimen Lesson Plan

Lesson: Collaborating on a Global Issue

Objective: Students collaborate with a global partner school on a shared issue.
Grade Level: 5–12
Materials: GFSC exchange platform (e.g., ePals), UN SDG resources, Google Docs.

Activities:

- (10 min) Introduce UN SDGs; show GFSC exchange platform.
- (25 min) Pairs: Draft a collaborative project plan with a partner school (e.g., water conservation, cultural preservation, sustainable energy).
- (15 min) Share plans; discuss cultural insights gained and challenges of global collaboration.
- (10 min) Reflection: Students write about how global collaboration helps solve complex problems and builds understanding.

Assessment: Evaluate plans for clarity; review reflections for global awareness.
Inclusivity: Provide offline exchange options; translate resources.

Chapter 8 Equity Inclusion

8. Equity and Inclusion: Building Schools for All Learners

Key Ideas: Education as a Universal Right

Enforcing equity audits and inclusive practices transforms global education by eliminating barriers, ensuring diverse students have equal access to quality learning.

- **Culturally Responsive Teaching (CRT):** Tailors instruction to honor students' cultural backgrounds, languages, and experiences. Includes diverse literature and indigenous perspectives.
- **Support Systems for Diverse Needs:** Robust support for students with disabilities (assistive technologies, IEPs) or economic challenges (devices, internet, supplies). GFSC offers free assistive software and NGO partnerships.
- **Transparent Policies to Address Bias:** Identify and address biases in school practices (discipline, grading, curriculum). Involves regular audits and community feedback.

Actionable Strategies: Building Inclusive Schools

- **Train Teachers in Culturally Responsive Pedagogy:** Use GFSC-curated training modules from organizations like Teaching Tolerance (Learning for Justice). *Timeline: 3-hour webinar series, ongoing.*
- **Provide Free or Subsidized Tech & Internet:** Partner with GFSC-linked NGOs for donated or subsidized tablets and portable Wi-Fi hotspots for low-income students. *Cost: ~$50 per tablet. Timeline: Pilot in 1 grade within 6 months.*

- **Create an Inclusion Task Force:** Form a task force with students, teachers, parents, and community members to audit school policies and curricula for equity gaps. *Timeline: Annual audits, ongoing.*
- **Develop Inclusive IEPs:** Use GFSC's free IEP templates to create tailored plans for students with disabilities, involving parents and specialists via virtual meetings. *Metric: 15% rise in academic inclusion.*

This chapter emphasizes creating inclusive schools that eliminate barriers for diverse learners through equity audits and culturally responsive teaching (CRT). It proposes training teachers using resources from organizations like Teaching Tolerance, providing subsidized tech devices and internet for low-income students, and forming inclusion task forces to audit curricula for bias. A specimen lesson plan encourages students to analyze their school's inclusivity and propose improvements, fostering ownership. CRT tailors instruction to reflect diverse identities, ensuring students feel valued. The chapter addresses systemic inequities, promoting justice and belonging through transparent policies and assistive technologies for students with disabilities. By aligning with 2025's focus on equity, it ensures accessibility for all, including non-English speakers and rural students. The broader impact is an education system that uplifts humanity by fostering compassionate, inclusive environments where every learner thrives. The GFSSC's role in funding scholarships and sharing resources ensures global scalability, creating schools that empower diverse populations and enhance social well-being through equitable education.

Broader Impact on Humanity and Well-Being

These key ideas transform education by creating inclusive, equitable environments that honor diversity and remove barriers. Culturally responsive teaching validates student identities. Support systems ensure universal access to education, narrowing opportunity gaps. Transparent policies address bias, building trust and fairness, empowering students to advocate for justice.

Policy Highlight

Enforce GFSC equity audits to ensure inclusive practices.

- Require annual audits of curricula and policies for cultural bias and accessibility.
- Provide GFSC-funded scholarships for devices and internet for low-income students.
- Train teachers on culturally responsive teaching via GFSC workshops.

Implementation Plan (10 months):

- **Q2 Year 2:** Develop equity audit templates with global diversity experts.
- **Q3 Year 2:** Train auditors via GFSC webinars.
- **Q4 Year 2:** Conduct pilot audits in 10 schools, results shared anonymously.
- **Q1 Year 3:** Mandate annual audits for all GFSC schools with GFSC-funded device scholarships.

Resource Sharing: Audit templates and inclusivity resources on GFSC platform. **Inclusivity:** Prioritize representation of marginalized groups in GFSC governance, translate materials.

Specimen Lesson Plan

Lesson: Auditing School Inclusivity

Objective: Students analyze their school's inclusivity and propose improvements.
Grade Level: 6–12
Materials: GFSC equity audit template, paper, access to school policies.

Activities:

- (10 min) Discuss GFSC audit template; define inclusivity.
- (25 min) Small groups: Conduct a mini-audit of school policies or spaces, using the template.
- (15 min) Groups present findings and one improvement idea.
- (10 min) Reflection: Students write about why equity is important in schools.

Assessment: Evaluate audits for thoroughness; assess reflections.
Inclusivity: Translate templates; support diverse input methods (e.g., audio).

Chapter 9 Teacher Facilitator

9. The Teacher as Facilitator: Redefining the Educator's Role

Key Ideas: Empowering Educators

Redefining teachers as facilitators transforms global education by empowering educators to guide student-led learning, fostering innovation and autonomy.

- **Teachers as Mentors:** Model curiosity and problem-solving, demonstrating how to ask questions, explore unknowns, and tackle challenges with resilience. GFSC provides free facilitation guides and inquiry-based lesson plans.
- **Co-Learning Opportunities:** Teachers and students explore new topics together, breaking traditional hierarchies and fostering mutual growth. Builds collaboration, encourages risk-taking, and models lifelong learning.
- **Professional Autonomy for Teachers:** Freedom to design creative, student-centered lessons without rigid mandates. Fosters job satisfaction and allows experimentation with methods like flipped classrooms.

Actionable Strategies: Elevating the Teaching Role

- **Offer Workshops on Facilitation Skills:** Focus on inquiry-based teaching methods, such as posing open-ended questions or modeling problem-solving steps. *Timeline: 2-hour webinar, ongoing.*
- **Encourage Teachers to Join Student Passion Projects:** Integrate co-learning where teachers participate in student-led explorations, researching alongside students. *Timeline: Weekly, ongoing.*

- **Provide Planning Time for Innovation:** Allocate one half-day monthly for teachers to design innovative lessons using GFSC's flexible frameworks. *Cost: Minimal (reallocate PD time). Timeline: Monthly, ongoing.*
- **Create Curiosity Journals:** Encourage teachers to document their questions and problem-solving processes, sharing excerpts with students to model curiosity. *Metric: 20% increase in teacher job satisfaction.*

This chapter redefines teachers as facilitators who guide student-led learning, modeling curiosity and problem-solving to foster innovation. It proposes forming peer-led learning communities, redefining teacher roles through GFSSC guidelines, and involving students in co-learning activities like joint research on trending topics (e.g., AI). Strategies include training teachers in inquiry-based methods, conducting equity audits for inclusive practices, and providing professional development via free online courses. A specimen lesson plan encourages students to lead lesson segments, practicing facilitation skills. The approach breaks traditional hierarchies, enhancing teacher motivation and student engagement. By aligning with 2025's focus on teacher-led innovation, it ensures inclusivity for diverse educators and learners, including those in low-tech settings. The broader impact is an education system that empowers educators to drive creativity and community engagement, fostering resilient, adaptive global societies. The GFSSC's role in sharing resources and training ensures scalability, creating vibrant learning environments where teachers and students collaborate to uplift humanity through curiosity and innovation.

Broader Impact on Humanity and Well-Being

These key ideas transform education by redefining teachers as empowered, collaborative facilitators. Teachers as mentors inspire curiosity and resilience. Co-learning opportunities build mutual respect and prepare students for collaborative careers. Professional autonomy unleashes teacher creativity, delivering engaging, relevant education.

Policy Highlight

Redefine teacher roles in GFSC schools as facilitators with autonomy.

- Develop GFSC guidelines for inquiry-based teaching and co-learning.
- Allocate 10% of teacher schedules for collaborative planning and innovation.
- Offer GFSC mentorship programs pairing novice and experienced facilitators.

Implementation Plan (9 months):

- **Q2 Year 2:** Develop GFSC facilitation guidelines.
- **Q3 Year 2:** Train teachers via GFSC webinars on inquiry-based methods.
- **Q4 Year 2:** Pilot facilitator roles in 10 schools, with mentorship programs established.
- **Q1 Year 3:** Scale to all GFSC schools, ensuring 10% of schedules for planning.

Resource Sharing: Facilitation training modules and videos on GFSC platform. **Inclusivity:** Training accessible in multiple formats for diverse educators.

Specimen Lesson Plan

Lesson: Students as Facilitators

Objective: Students lead a lesson segment, practicing facilitation skills.
Grade Level: 7–12
Materials: GFSC facilitation guide, topic list (e.g., math concept), whiteboard.

Activities:

- (10 min) Explain facilitation roles using GFSC guide; model inquiry-based questions.
- (25 min) Pairs: Prepare and deliver a 5-minute lesson on a chosen topic.
- (15 min) Class feedback: What made the facilitation effective?
- (10 min) Reflection: Students write about how leading felt.

Assessment: Evaluate facilitation for engagement; review reflections.
Inclusivity: Allow diverse presentation formats; translate guides.

Chapter 10 Lifelong Learning

10. Lifelong Learning: Fostering a Culture of Continuous Growth

Key Ideas: Empowering Continuous Growth

Instilling lifelong learning skills transforms global education by equipping students with tools for continuous growth, ensuring adaptability in a changing world.

- **Teach Independent Learning:** Equip students to navigate and utilize online resources effectively (e.g., Coursera, edX, Khan Academy). Develops digital literacy, time management, and critical evaluation.
- **Emphasize Growth Mindset Principles:** Belief that abilities can improve through effort and learning. Encourages students to embrace challenges, persist through setbacks, and view failures as opportunities.
- **Alumni Networks:** Connect current students with graduates as mentors, sharing expertise, career advice, or learning resources. Fosters community, provides role models, and bridges generational knowledge gaps.

Actionable Strategies: Cultivating Adaptability

- **Introduce Students to Platforms like Coursera or edX:** Incorporate GFSC-recommended platforms for self-directed courses (e.g., "Introduction to Python"). *Cost: ~$100 for classroom computer. Timeline: Pilot in 1 subject within 3 months.*
- **Incorporate Growth Mindset Lessons:** Use GFSC-curated Mindset Works activities into weekly advisory periods (e.g., journaling about challenges overcome). *Cost: Minimal. Timeline: Weekly, ongoing.*

- **Create an Alumni Mentorship Program:** Establish a GFSC-guided program connecting alumni with students via virtual platforms (e.g., Zoom, email). *Timeline: Monthly meetings, ongoing.*
- **Develop Resource Navigation Lessons:** Dedicate one class monthly to GFSC-designed lessons on evaluating online resources (e.g., checking source credibility). *Metric: 15% increase in student self-efficacy.*

This chapter promotes a culture of lifelong learning by equipping students with independent learning skills and a growth mindset, encouraging resilience and adaptability. It advocates for access to free online platforms like Coursera, establishing alumni mentorship programs, and creating global learning networks to share knowledge. Strategies include forming GFSC-supported learning communities, encouraging student-led exploration through passion projects, and providing offline resources for low-tech schools. A specimen lesson plan guides students to explore self-directed learning using online platforms, fostering autonomy. The approach aligns with 2025's demand for continuous learning, addressing gaps for underserved students. By teaching students how to learn independently, it prepares them for dynamic careers and personal growth. The broader impact is an education system that empowers individuals to pursue knowledge lifelong, enhancing global resilience and opportunity. The GFSSC's role in providing free, multilingual resources ensures accessibility, creating a connected, innovative world where every learner thrives through autonomy and a commitment to growth.

Broader Impact on Humanity and Well-Being

These key ideas transform education by fostering a culture of continuous, self-directed growth. Independent learning equips students to navigate an evolving world. Growth mindset builds resilience and optimism. Alumni networks create enduring support systems, strengthening community bonds and providing access to opportunities.

Policy Highlight

Establish a Global Future School Consortium (GFSC) to collaboratively define and promote a shared vision for transformative education.

- Curate free lifelong learning resources (e.g., Coursera, edX) on the GFSC platform.
- Integrate growth mindset lessons into advisory periods, using free Mindset Works resources.
- Pilot alumni mentorship networks in 10 schools, facilitated via WhatsApp or email.

Implementation Plan (9 months):

- **Q2 Year 2:** Curate free lifelong learning resources on GFSC platform.
- **Q3 Year 2:** Integrate growth mindset lessons into advisory periods.
- **Q4 Year 2:** Pilot alumni mentorship networks in 10 schools.
- **Q1 Year 3:** Scale to all GFSC schools, with offline learning kits for low-tech areas.

Resource Sharing: Resources and lesson plans on GFSC platform. **Inclusivity:** Offline kits and multilingual resources.

Specimen Lesson Plan

Lesson: Exploring Self-Directed Learning

Objective: Students explore self-directed learning using online platforms.
Grade Level: 5–12
Materials: Access to Coursera or edX, GFSC growth mindset resources, notebooks.

Activities:

- (10 min) Introduce growth mindset using GFSC resources; demo Coursera.
- (25 min) Students select a free course and outline a learning plan.
- (15 min) Share plans in pairs; discuss motivation.
- (10 min) Reflection: Students write about how lifelong learning will help them.

Assessment: Evaluate plans for clarity; assess reflections.
Inclusivity: Provide offline course summaries; translate resources.

Chapter 11 STEAM

11. STEAM Education: Integrating Arts with Science and Technology

Key Ideas: Holistic Creativity and Innovation

Integrating STEAM globally transforms education by blending arts with STEM, fostering creativity and innovation through cost-effective maker spaces and shared interdisciplinary projects.

- **Interdisciplinary Projects:** Combine coding with visual art or music with physics. Students code animations, or compose music to demonstrate physics concepts, fostering connections across disciplines.
- **Maker Spaces:** Dedicated areas with tools like 3D printers, craft supplies, and recycled materials for hands-on STEAM exploration. Students build prototypes or artworks, learning through trial and error.
- **Community Artist Partnerships:** Local artists enrich curricula through workshops or collaborative projects (e.g., a muralist leading a workshop on public art). Exposes students to creative careers and fosters community pride.

Actionable Strategies: Fostering Creative Innovation

- **Integrate Art into Science Lessons:** Use GFSC-provided lesson plans to incorporate art, such as designing infographics for climate data. *Cost: ~$200 for a classroom computer. Timeline: One project per quarter.*
- **Set Up a Low-Cost Maker Space:** Establish a maker space in a classroom corner using GFSC blueprints, with a budget 3D printer, donated craft supplies, and recycled

materials. *Cost: ~$300 for 3D printer. Timeline: Pilot in 1 classroom within 6 months.*

- **Invite Local Artists for Workshops:** Fund workshops with small community grants or crowdfunding. A potter leads a workshop on clay modeling, linking to physics. *Cost: ~$200 per workshop. Timeline: Quarterly.*
- **Launch Coding-Art Challenges:** Organize monthly GFSC-guided challenges where students code visual art (e.g., geometric patterns in Python). *Metric: 20% increase in student creativity.*

This chapter champions STEAM education by integrating arts with STEM to foster creativity, innovation, and holistic thinking. It proposes dedicating 30% of GFSSC curricula to STEAM, using open-source project templates and low-cost maker spaces to create hands-on learning environments. Strategies include inviting local artists for workshops, hosting STEAM fairs, and developing interdisciplinary projects like designing sustainable products. A specimen lesson plan guides students to plan a school sustainability initiative, blending art and science. The approach ensures accessibility for diverse learners, including those in rural areas, by using minimal technology and offline resources. By aligning with 2025's focus on innovative skills, STEAM education prepares students for real-world challenges like sustainability. The broader impact is an education system that cultivates inventive thinking and resilience, fostering equitable access to opportunities. The GFSSC's role in sharing free templates and training teachers ensures global scalability, creating inclusive environments where students develop practical skills and contribute to a creative, sustainable world.

Broader Impact on Humanity and Well-Being

These key ideas transform education by integrating arts and STEM, creating inclusive, creative learning environments. Interdisciplinary projects foster innovative thinking, preparing students to solve complex issues. Maker spaces encourage hands-on exploration, building resilience and practical skills. Community artist partnerships celebrate cultural diversity, strengthening community bonds.

Policy Highlight

Mandate STEAM integration in 30% of GFSC curricula.

- Develop open-source STEAM project templates combining art and science.
- Create low-cost maker spaces using recycled materials.
- Partner with global artists for virtual workshops.

Implementation Plan (10 months):

- **Q2 Year 2:** Develop STEAM project templates, shared on GFSC platform.
- **Q3 Year 2:** Pilot maker spaces in 10 schools, using recycled materials.
- **Q4 Year 2:** Train teachers via GFSC webinars on STEAM integration.
- **Q1 Year 3:** Scale to all GFSC schools, with virtual artist workshops.

Resource Sharing: STEAM project guides and maker space plans on GFSC platform.
Inclusivity: Projects reflect diverse cultural art forms.

Specimen Lesson Plan

Lesson: Planning a Sustainable School Initiative (STEAM)

Objective: Students plan a school sustainability initiative, integrating STEAM concepts.
Grade Level: 5–12
Materials: GFSC sustainability guide, NASA climate resources, poster paper, recycled materials.

Activities:

- (10 min) Discuss climate change using NASA resources; introduce GFSC guide.
- (25 min) Groups: Plan a sustainability project (e.g., composting program, solar-powered model) integrating science, art, and engineering.
- (15 min) Groups present plans to class, showcasing their creative solutions.
- (10 min) Reflection: Students write about how schools can lead sustainability through STEAM.

Assessment: Evaluate plans for feasibility and creativity; assess reflections.
Inclusivity: Adapt projects for local environments; translate guides.

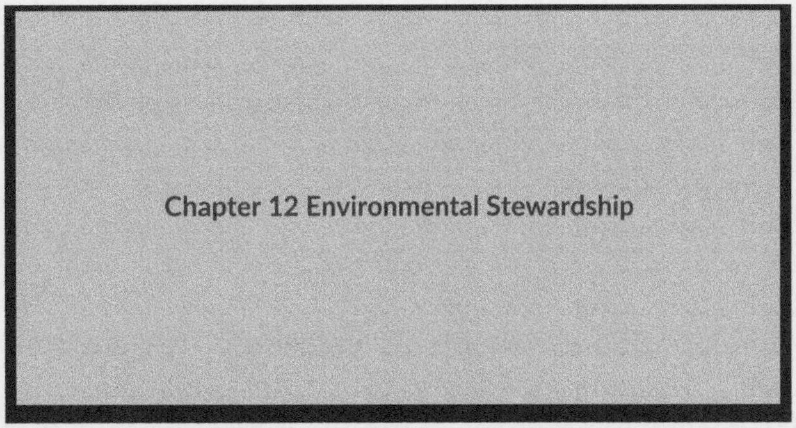

12. Environmental Stewardship: Schools as Hubs for Sustainability

Key Ideas: Schools as Sustainability Hubs

Positioning schools as sustainability hubs transforms global education by embedding environmental responsibility, preparing students to tackle climate challenges.

- **School Gardens and Composting Programs:** Hands-on learning for sustainable practices (soil health, biodiversity, waste reduction). Students grow crops, calculate water needs, and compost food scraps.
- **Energy-Efficient Facilities as Learning Tools:** Solar panels, rainwater harvesting, or LED lighting demonstrate renewable energy. Students monitor energy output or water collection, applying math and science.
- **Curricula Focused on Environmental Justice and Climate Solutions:** Explore how pollution impacts marginalized communities and cover solutions like renewable energy. Fosters critical thinking and civic engagement.

Actionable Strategies: Cultivating Eco-Conscious Citizens

- **Start a School Garden with Community Donations:** Launch a garden using GFSC blueprints, with donated seeds and tools. Students plant, maintain, and harvest crops. *Cost: ~$100 for 100 sq ft garden. Timeline: Pilot within 3 months.*
- **Install Solar Panels or Rainwater Systems as Teaching Aids:** Pilot one small solar panel or rainwater barrel. Students monitor outputs weekly, analyzing data. *Cost:*

~$200 for solar panel. Timeline: Pilot within 6 months.

- **Integrate Climate Change Topics into Science & Social Studies:** Use GFSC-curated NASA resources to analyze global temperature data or study climate migration. *Timeline: Weekly lessons, ongoing.*
- **Establish Garden Clubs:** Create student-led clubs to manage gardens and teach peers, fostering leadership and sustainability. *Metric: 20% reduction in school energy use within 1 year.*

This chapter positions schools as epicenters for environmental stewardship, teaching students to address climate challenges through sustainable practices. It proposes starting school gardens with community donations, retrofitting facilities for energy efficiency, and embedding environmental justice in 15% of science and social studies curricula. Strategies include student-led eco-audits, partnerships with green organizations, and using GFSSC blueprints for low-cost sustainability projects. A specimen lesson plan encourages students to plan a sustainability initiative, fostering advocacy. The approach enhances mental health through outdoor engagement and aligns with 2025's climate goals, ensuring accessibility with offline resources. The broader impact is a global education system that equips students to tackle environmental issues, promoting eco-conscious communities and equitable solutions. The GFSSC's role in sharing scalable frameworks ensures even resource-constrained schools can adopt these practices, fostering a compassionate, sustainable world where students lead climate action and contribute to global well-being.

Broader Impact on Humanity and Well-Being

These key ideas transform schools into hubs of sustainability. Gardens and composting cultivate practical skills, reducing waste and promoting food security. Energy-efficient facilities model green technologies, inspiring innovation. Curricula on environmental justice empower students to tackle inequities and propose solutions.

Policy Highlight

Require GFSC schools to adopt sustainable practices.

- Implement school gardens and composting programs with GFSC funding.
- Use energy-efficient systems as teaching tools.
- Integrate environmental justice into curricula.

Implementation Plan (10 months):

- **Q2 Year 2:** Develop sustainability guides for gardens and energy systems.
- **Q3 Year 2:** Fund pilot gardens in 10 schools via GFSC grants and local donations.
- **Q4 Year 2:** Integrate environmental justice into curricula, using free NASA resources.
- **Q1 Year 3:** Scale to all GFSC schools, with virtual tours of sustainable facilities.

Resource Sharing: Sustainability guides and case studies on GFSC platform. **Inclusivity:** Adapt practices for urban and rural contexts.

Specimen Lesson Plan

Lesson: Planning a School Sustainability Initiative

Objective: Students plan a school sustainability initiative.
Grade Level: 5–12
Materials: GFSC sustainability guide, NASA climate resources, poster paper, notebooks.

Activities:

- (10 min) Discuss climate change using NASA resources; introduce GFSC guide.
- (25 min) Groups: Plan a sustainability project (e.g., composting program, school energy audit, water conservation system).
- (15 min) Groups present plans to class, explaining their environmental impact.
- (10 min) Reflection: Students write about how schools can lead sustainability efforts in their communities.

Assessment: Evaluate plans for feasibility; assess reflections.
Inclusivity: Adapt projects for local environments; translate guides.

Chapter 13 Digital Literacy

13. Digital Literacy: Navigating the Information Age with Confidence

Key Ideas: Empowering Digital Citizens

Mandating digital literacy transforms global education by equipping students with critical skills to navigate technology ethically, ensuring universal access.

- **Lessons on Spotting Misinformation and Bias:** Equip students to critically evaluate digital content, identify red flags, and use fact-checking tools. Integrates into social studies or English.
- **Coding as a Core Skill:** Foundational skill enabling students to create digital solutions (apps, games, websites). Platforms like Code.org offer free, beginner-friendly courses.
- **Cybersecurity Basics:** Teach students to protect their digital identities through practices like strong passwords, secure privacy settings, and phishing awareness. Critical for safe online behavior.

Actionable Strategies: Navigating the Digital World

- **Use Free Resources from Common Sense Media:** Implement GFSC-curated lesson plans for weekly media literacy sessions. Students analyze articles or videos using GFSC checklists. *Cost: Minimal. Timeline: Weekly lessons, ongoing.*

- **Introduce Coding via Platforms like Code.org:** Implement GFSC-guided Code.org curricula, starting with one hour weekly for grades K-12. *Cost: ~$100 for shared tablet. Timeline: Weekly lessons, ongoing.*
- **Host Annual "Digital Safety Days":** Organize GFSC-guided workshops teaching students to secure accounts and avoid phishing. Includes role-playing exercises. *Cost: ~$50 for materials. Timeline: Annually.*
- **Create Fact-Checking Clubs:** Establish student-led clubs to investigate local misinformation, fostering leadership and peer education. *Metric: 20% increase in student ability to identify misinformation.*

This chapter advocates for digital literacy as a core subject to equip students with ethical navigation skills in the information age. It proposes teaching media literacy, cybersecurity, and coding through student-led fact-checking clubs and annual hackathons using platforms like Code.org. Strategies include mandating digital literacy in GFSSC schools, integrating 5-minute cybersecurity tips into classes, and ensuring offline resources for accessibility. A specimen lesson plan guides students to evaluate online information for credibility, fostering critical thinking. The approach aligns with 2025's tech demands, addressing issues like AI-generated misinformation and automation skills. By prioritizing ethical digital use, it ensures safety and inclusivity for diverse learners, including those in low-connectivity areas. The broader impact is an education system that empowers students to thrive in a digital world, promoting global social responsibility. The GFSSC's role in providing free, multilingual resources ensures universal access, creating confident, informed citizens who navigate technology responsibly.

Broader Impact on Humanity and Well-Being

These key ideas transform education by fostering digital literacy, empowering students to navigate the information age with confidence and responsibility. Lessons on misinformation combat false information, strengthening democratic processes. Coding unlocks economic opportunities. Cybersecurity ensures safe online engagement, protecting personal and community well-being.

Policy Highlight

Mandate digital literacy as a core GFSC subject.

- Teach media literacy and cybersecurity starting in elementary school.
- Use free platforms like Code.org for coding instruction.
- Host GFSC-led "Digital Safety Days" annually.

Implementation Plan (9 months):

- **Q2 Year 2:** Develop digital literacy curricula using free resources from Common Sense Media.
- **Q3 Year 2:** Pilot curricula in 10 schools, including coding via Code.org.
- **Q4 Year 2:** Host "Digital Safety Days" via Zoom, with global participation.
- **Q1 Year 3:** Scale to all GFSC schools, with offline coding kits for low-tech areas.

Resource Sharing: Digital literacy curricula and videos on GFSC platform. **Inclusivity:** Multilingual and offline resources.

Specimen Lesson Plan

Lesson: Evaluating Online Information

Objective: Students evaluate online information for credibility.
Grade Level: 6–12
Materials: GFSC digital literacy curriculum, Common Sense Media resources, internet access.

Activities:

- (10 min) Discuss misinformation using GFSC curriculum examples.
- (25 min) Pairs: Analyze a website for credibility, using a GFSC checklist.
- (15 min) Share findings; discuss red flags and common biases.
- (10 min) Reflection: Students write about why digital literacy is critical for informed decision-making.

Assessment: Evaluate analyses for accuracy; review reflections.
Inclusivity: Provide offline checklists; translate resources.

Chapter 14 Collaborative Learning

14. Collaborative Learning: The Power of Peer-to-Peer Education

Key Ideas: Fostering Teamwork and Communication

Prioritizing collaborative learning transforms global education by fostering teamwork and communication, leveraging shared tools to create inclusive, peer-driven learning experiences.

- **Group Projects with Defined Roles:** Teach accountability by ensuring equitable participation and shared responsibility (e.g., leader, scribe, researcher). Integrates subjects and mirrors real-world teamwork.
- **Peer Tutoring Programs:** Pair older or more advanced students with younger or struggling peers. Reinforces learning for both tutor and tutee, fostering communication and empathy.
- **Online Collaboration Tools:** Enable students to work together in real-time, whether in class or remotely (e.g., Google Docs, Microsoft Teams). Develops digital fluency and teamwork.

Actionable Strategies: Empowering Peer Education

- **Assign Group Roles in Projects:** Implement GFSC-guided group projects, assigning roles for weekly tasks (e.g., creating a digital poster on renewable energy). *Timeline: Weekly, ongoing.*
- **Create a Peer Tutoring System:** Pair older students with younger ones for weekly 30-minute sessions in subjects like math or literacy. Use GFSC training modules. *Cost:*

Minimal. Timeline: Pilot in 1 grade pair within 3 months.

- **Use Google Docs or Microsoft Teams:** Implement GFSC-guided projects using these tools for collaborative assignments (e.g., shared history timeline). *Cost: ~$200 for classroom computer. Timeline: 1-2 projects per semester.*
- **Host Collaboration Showcases:** Organize quarterly GFSC-guided events where groups present projects (e.g., a model eco-village). *Metric: 25% improvement in student teamwork skills.*

This chapter emphasizes collaborative learning to foster teamwork, communication, and peer-driven innovation. It proposes dedicating 15% of GFSSC instructional time to group projects, using tools like Google Docs and Microsoft Teams, and awarding tutoring badges to motivate participation. Strategies include hosting quarterly collaboration showcases, creating global team projects via GFSSC platforms, and training students as peer tutors. A specimen lesson plan guides students to collaborate on projects with defined roles, enhancing teamwork skills. The approach aligns with 2025's focus on collaborative innovation, addressing post-COVID educational gaps. By ensuring accessibility with offline rubrics, it supports diverse learners, including those in remote areas. The broader impact is an education system that prepares students for collaborative careers in fields like technology and NGOs, fostering social cohesion. The GFSSC's role in facilitating virtual platforms and low-cost resources ensures global scalability, creating inclusive, peer-driven learning environments that uplift humanity through teamwork and shared growth.

Broader Impact on Humanity and Well-Being

These key ideas transform education by harnessing peer-to-peer collaboration, fostering skills essential for a connected, cooperative world. Group projects build accountability and teamwork. Peer tutoring programs enhance learning and empathy, reducing educational disparities. Online collaboration tools bridge geographic and cultural divides.

Policy Highlight

Require 15% of GFSC instructional time for collaborative learning.

- Implement group projects with defined roles for accountability.
- Establish peer tutoring programs across grade levels.
- Use free collaboration tools like Google Docs.

Implementation Plan (9 months):

- **Q2 2026:** Develop collaboration frameworks with role-based project templates.
- **Q3 2026:** Pilot peer tutoring programs in 10 schools, using Google Docs.
- **Q4 2026:** Train teachers via GFSC webinars on facilitating group work.
- **Q1 2027:** Scale to all GFSC schools, with feedback shared globally.

Resource Sharing: Collaboration frameworks and tools on GFSC platform. **Inclusivity:** Group roles accommodate diverse abilities and languages.

Specimen Lesson Plan

Lesson: Collaborative Project with Roles

Objective: Students collaborate on a group project with defined roles.
Grade Level: 4–10
Materials: GFSC collaboration framework, Google Docs, topic list.

Activities:

- (10 min) Introduce GFSC framework; assign roles (e.g., leader, scribe, researcher, presenter).
- (25 min) Groups: Create a presentation on a chosen topic (e.g., local history, a scientific discovery, a social issue).
- (15 min) Groups present to class; discuss teamwork dynamics and challenges faced.
- (10 min) Reflection: Students write about how collaboration helped them achieve their project goals.

Assessment: Evaluate presentations for role clarity and content; assess reflections.
Inclusivity: Adapt roles for diverse abilities; translate frameworks.

Chapter 15 Mental Health

15. Mental Health Matters: Supporting Student Well-Being

Key Ideas: Prioritizing Well-Being

Embedding mental health resources transforms global education by creating supportive environments that prioritize student well-being, enhancing resilience.

- **On-Site Counsellors and Mental Health Workshops:** Provide professional mental health support and educate students on coping strategies (e.g., mindfulness, goal-setting). Reduces stigma and promotes help-seeking.
- **Safe Spaces for Students:** Quiet, welcoming environments (e.g., "calm rooms") to process stress or trauma. Equipped with comfortable seating, calming visuals, and mindfulness resources.
- **Curriculum Integration of Stress Management:** Embed techniques like deep breathing, progressive muscle relaxation, or time management into daily lessons. Normalizes mental health practices and builds resilience.

Actionable Strategies: Fostering Resilience

- **Partner with Local Mental Health Organizations:** Secure one on-site counsellor for weekly visits at no or minimal cost. Counsellors provide individual sessions or group workshops. *Cost: ~$50/month (subsidized). Timeline: Pilot in 1 grade within 6 months.*
- **Create a "Calm Room":** Set up a calm room in an unused classroom or corner with donated cushions and GFSC's free mindfulness resources. *Cost: ~$50 for cushions.*

Timeline: Pilot within 3 months.

- **Train Teachers to Incorporate Stress-Relief Activities:** Use GFSC lesson plans to integrate 2-5 minute stress-relief activities daily (e.g., deep breathing before tests). *Cost: Minimal. Timeline: Daily, ongoing.*
- **Host Mental Health Awareness Weeks:** Organize GFSC-guided events with guest speakers from partner organizations, addressing topics like anxiety. *Metric: 25% reduction in behavioral issues.*

This chapter prioritizes student mental health by embedding resources like safe spaces, mindfulness exercises, and stress management curricula into schools. It proposes hosting mental health awareness weeks, training student ambassadors to guide peers, and integrating stress-relief techniques into daily routines. Strategies include mandating mental health resources in GFSSC schools, using offline workbooks for accessibility, and partnering with NGOs for community-based solutions. A specimen lesson plan guides students to practice mindfulness techniques, fostering resilience. The approach aligns with 2025's focus on addressing digital and environmental stress, ensuring inclusivity for diverse learners, including non-native speakers. By creating supportive environments, it reduces anxiety and enhances focus, promoting academic and social success. The broader impact is a global education system that nurtures resilient, empathetic students equipped to handle life's challenges. The GFSSC's role in providing culturally adapted, low-cost resources ensures scalability, fostering harmonious communities worldwide through mental health-focused education.

Broader Impact on Humanity and Well-Being

These key ideas transform schools into sanctuaries of mental health support. Counsellors and workshops provide accessible care, reducing stigma. Safe spaces offer refuge for processing stress or trauma. Curriculum-integrated stress management equips students with lifelong coping skills, mitigating global stressors.

Policy Highlight

Mandate GFSC schools to provide mental health resources.

- Partner with NGOs for free or low-cost counseling services.
- Create "calm rooms" with GFSC-provided design guides.
- Train teachers on mental health awareness via GFSC webinars.

Implementation Plan (10 months):

- **Q2 Year 2:** Partner with NGOs (e.g., Mental Health International) for free counseling resources.
- **Q3 Year 2:** Pilot "calm rooms" in 10 schools, using GFSC design guides.
- **Q4 Year 2:** Train teachers on mental health awareness via GFSC webinars.
- **Q1 Year 3:** Scale to all GFSC schools, with offline mindfulness guides.

Resource Sharing: Mindfulness and counseling resources on GFSC platform. **Inclusivity:** Translate resources and train counselors for diverse cultural needs.

Specimen Lesson Plan

Lesson: Practicing Mindfulness for Stress Management

Objective: Students practice a mindfulness technique to manage stress.
Grade Level: 3–12
Materials: GFSC mindfulness guide, quiet space, optional Calm app access.

Activities:

- (10 min) Introduce mindfulness using GFSC guide; model deep breathing.
- (20 min) Practice a 5-minute guided mindfulness exercise.
- (20 min) Discuss: How did it feel? Share stress management tips.
- (10 min) Reflection: Students write about how mindfulness can help daily life.

Assessment: Observe participation; evaluate reflections.
Inclusivity: Offer non-verbal reflection options; translate guides.

Chapter 16 Future Assessment

16. The Future of Assessment: Beyond Standardised Tests

Key Ideas: Authentic and Equitable Evaluation

Shifting to competency-based assessments transforms global education by measuring real-world skills authentically, ensuring equitable, meaningful evaluations.

- **Portfolios Showcasing Student Work:** Digital or physical compilations of essays, projects, videos, or reflections. Provide a holistic view of growth and competencies, capturing diverse skills like critical thinking.
- **Performance-Based Tasks:** Assess practical skills like communication, problem-solving, and innovation through presentations, prototypes, or simulations. Replaces traditional tests with authentic evaluations.
- **Real-Time Feedback Systems:** Provide instant insights during lessons (e.g., apps, teacher check-ins), enabling students to improve immediately. Enhances learning agility and boosts confidence.

Actionable Strategies: Rethinking Evaluation

- **Implement Digital Portfolios:** Use GFSC-guided Google Sites or Seesaw to create digital portfolios for grades 3-12, updated monthly with student work. *Cost: ~$200 for classroom computer. Timeline: Pilot in 1 subject within 3 months.*
- **Replace Some Tests with Project-Based Assessments:** Implement GFSC-guided performance tasks, replacing one test per quarter with projects like designing a community health campaign. *Timeline: 1-2 per quarter, ongoing.*

- **Use Apps Like Socrative for Instant Feedback:** Implement GFSC-guided Socrative quizzes for weekly lessons, providing real-time feedback in subjects like math or science. *Cost: ~$100 for shared tablet. Timeline: Weekly, ongoing.*
- **Create Community Panels:** Invite local leaders to evaluate student presentations, providing real-world feedback. *Metric: 15% improvement in student practical skills.*

This chapter reimagines assessment by replacing 50% of traditional tests with competency-based evaluations, such as digital portfolios and real-time feedback systems. It proposes hosting quarterly portfolio showcases, inviting community panels to evaluate student work, and using GFSSC templates for accessibility in low-tech schools. A specimen lesson plan guides students to create portfolio entries, fostering self-assessment. The approach aligns with 2025's demand for practical, competency-based credentials, ensuring relevance for diverse learners. Strategies include developing feedback workshops to teach students goal-setting and using apps like Socrative for instant feedback. By emphasizing authentic assessments like presentations and prototypes, it prepares students for real-world challenges. The broader impact is an education system that values skills over rote memorization, promoting equity and engagement. The GFSSC's role in providing free, scalable tools ensures global accessibility, creating inclusive assessment practices that uplift humanity by recognizing diverse talents and fostering lifelong learning.

Broader Impact on Humanity and Well-Being

These key ideas transform assessment by prioritizing authentic, equitable evaluations. Portfolios showcase diverse talents and growth, fostering agency. Performance-based tasks align education with practical demands, cultivating innovation. Real-time feedback systems promote resilience and immediate growth, supporting diverse learners.

Policy Highlight

Replace 50% of traditional tests with competency-based assessments in GFSC schools.

- Implement digital portfolios using free platforms like Seesaw.
- Develop GFSC rubrics for project-based assessments.
- Train teachers on real-time feedback systems.

Implementation Plan (9 months):

- **Q2 Year 2:** Develop digital portfolio templates using Seesaw.
- **Q3 Year 2:** Pilot portfolio-based assessments in 10 schools, with GFSC rubrics.
- **Q4 Year 2:** Train teachers on real-time feedback via GFSC webinars.
- **Q1 Year 3:** Scale to all GFSC schools, with offline portfolio options.

Resource Sharing: Portfolio templates and rubrics on GFSC platform. **Inclusivity:** Assessments accommodate diverse learning needs and languages.

Specimen Lesson Plan

Lesson: Creating a Portfolio Entry

Objective: Students create a portfolio entry to showcase learning.
Grade Level: 5–12
Materials: GFSC portfolio template, Seesaw or Google Sites, project samples.

Activities:

- (10 min) Introduce portfolio assessment using GFSC template; show examples of strong portfolio entries.
- (25 min) Students create a portfolio entry (e.g., project summary, reflection on a skill, creative piece).
- (15 min) Share entries in pairs; provide peer feedback using a GFSC rubric.
- (10 min) Reflection: Students write about why portfolios are meaningful for demonstrating their learning journey.

Assessment: Evaluate entries for depth and alignment with learning objectives; review reflections.
Inclusivity: Offer offline portfolio options; translate templates.

17. Community Engagement: Schools as Civic and Cultural Hubs

Key Ideas: Schools as Community Pillars

Positioning schools as community hubs transforms global education by fostering civic engagement and cultural pride, connecting schools with local and global partners.

- **Community Service Integrated into Curricula:** Embeds civic responsibility into education. Students tutor younger peers or organize park cleanups, aligning with subjects like social studies or science.
- **Local Businesses as Learning Partners:** Internships or career shadowing days connect students with real-world work environments. Students shadow a baker or intern at a tech startup, learning practical skills.
- **Public Events to Showcase Student Work:** Art exhibitions, science fairs, or performances display student projects, fostering community pride and engagement. Strengthens school-community bonds.

Actionable Strategies: Building Stronger Communities

- **Require Community Service Hours Tied to Academic Projects:** Implement GFSC-guided service projects (e.g., tutoring elementary students in literacy or math). *Timeline: 10 hours per semester, ongoing.*

- **Partner with Local Businesses for Career Shadowing Days:** Use GFSC outreach templates to connect with businesses for one-day shadowing programs for grades 9-12. *Timeline: Annually.*
- **Host Monthly "Community Nights":** Organize GFSC-guided events showcasing student projects (e.g., recycled art display, history skit). *Cost: ~$50 for materials. Timeline: Monthly.*
- **Create Service Portfolios:** Have students compile service experiences in GFSC-supported portfolios, showcasing impact and reflections. *Metric: 20% increase in parental involvement.*

This chapter positions schools as civic and cultural hubs, fostering partnerships with communities to enhance engagement and cultural pride. It proposes creating service portfolios, developing internship pipelines with local businesses, and hosting digital galleries to showcase student work. Strategies include mandating quarterly community events, integrating service into curricula, and using GFSSC templates for event planning. A specimen lesson plan guides students to plan community events, promoting civic responsibility. The approach aligns with 2025's emphasis on community-driven education, ensuring inclusivity for diverse families through translated materials and virtual options. By connecting schools with local and global partners, it bridges cultural gaps and fosters pride in heritage. The broader impact is an education system that strengthens community ties, preparing students for active citizenship. The GFSSC's role in sharing resources and facilitating partnerships ensures scalability, creating vibrant, inclusive hubs that uplift humanity through collaboration and cultural celebration.

Broader Impact on Humanity and Well-Being

These key ideas transform schools into civic and cultural hubs. Community service empowers students to address local challenges. Partnerships with local businesses provide career exposure, reducing economic disparities. Public events celebrate student achievements, fostering pride and cultural unity.

Policy Highlight

Require GFSC schools to host quarterly community events.

- Integrate community service into curricula with GFSC guidelines.
- Partner with local businesses for career exploration programs.
- Host "Community Nights" to showcase student work.

Implementation Plan (10 months):

- **Q2 Year 2:** Develop event planning guides.
- **Q3 Year 2:** Pilot "Community Nights" in 10 schools, funded by local donations.
- **Q4 Year 2:** Partner with businesses for career exploration programs, facilitated via GFSC.
- **Q1 Year 3:** Scale to all GFSC schools, with virtual event options.

Resource Sharing: Event planning guides and partnership templates on GFSC platform.
Inclusivity: Engage diverse community groups in event planning.

Specimen Lesson Plan

Lesson: Planning a Community Showcase

Objective: Students plan a community event to showcase learning.
Grade Level: 6–12
Materials: GFSC event planning guide, poster paper, local contact list.

Activities:

- (10 min) Introduce GFSC guide; show past community event examples.
- (25 min) Groups: Plan a "Community Night" event (e.g., student project showcase, cultural festival, local issue awareness fair).
- (15 min) Groups present plans to class, detailing logistics and community benefits.
- (10 min) Reflection: Students write about how community engagement strengthens schools and benefits society.

Assessment: Evaluate plans for feasibility; assess reflections.
Inclusivity: Include diverse community voices; translate guides.

Chapter 18 Entrepreneurial

18. Entrepreneurial Mindsets: Fostering Innovation and Risk-Taking

Key Ideas: Cultivating Innovation and Resilience

Promoting entrepreneurial mindsets transforms global education by fostering creativity, resilience, and risk-taking to solve real-world problems.

- **Student-Led "Start-Up" Projects:** Students identify and address local challenges (e.g., food waste, lack of green spaces) by designing innovative solutions, mimicking entrepreneurial processes.
- **Workshops on Financial Literacy and Innovation:** Teach essential skills like budgeting, investing, and creative problem-solving. GFSC provides free resources from Junior Achievement.
- **Mentorship from Local Entrepreneurs:** Provides students with real-world insights, inspiration, and guidance. Tech founders or small business owners mentor students on projects or discuss strategies.

Actionable Strategies: Preparing for a Dynamic Future

- **Create a "Shark Tank"-Style Event:** Organize quarterly events where student teams pitch start-up ideas (e.g., community composting app) to local judges. *Cost: ~$50 for materials. Timeline: Quarterly.*

- **Use Free Financial Literacy Resources from Junior Achievement:** Implement GFSC-curated workshops monthly, covering topics like budgeting or market research. *Cost: Minimal. Timeline: Monthly, ongoing.*
- **Invite Local Entrepreneurs for Guest Lectures:** Invite 2-4 entrepreneurs annually for guest lectures via Zoom or in person, discussing topics like risk-taking or market analysis. *Cost: Minimal. Timeline: Annually.*
- **Launch Start-Up Incubators:** Create GFSC-supported student clubs to refine projects year-round, fostering sustained innovation. *Metric: 15% increase in student problem-solving skills.*

This chapter promotes entrepreneurial education to cultivate innovation, risk-taking, and financial literacy among students. It proposes hosting innovation challenges, offering mentorship from local and global entrepreneurs, and integrating financial literacy workshops using free resources. Strategies include mandating entrepreneurial education in GFSSC schools, creating start-up pitch events, and using GFSSC templates for project guidance. A specimen lesson plan guides students to pitch solutions for school issues, fostering creativity. The approach aligns with 2025's demand for youth-driven solutions, addressing economic volatility through practical skills. By ensuring accessibility with offline guides and low-cost materials, it supports diverse learners, including those in rural areas. The broader impact is an education system that prepares students for dynamic careers, fostering resilience and innovation. The GFSSC's role in connecting schools with global mentors and sharing resources ensures scalability, creating a world where students drive economic and social progress through entrepreneurial thinking.

Broader Impact on Humanity and Well-Being

These key ideas transform education by fostering entrepreneurial mindsets. Student-led start-up projects empower students to solve local problems. Financial literacy and innovation workshops provide tools for economic independence. Mentorship from local entrepreneurs inspires ambition and connects education to real-world opportunities.

Policy Highlight

Mandate entrepreneurial education in GFSC schools.

- Implement student-led "start-up" projects with GFSC templates.
- Offer financial literacy workshops using free resources.
- Connect with global entrepreneurs for virtual mentorship.

Implementation Plan (9 months):

- **Q2 Year 2:** Develop "start-up" project templates.
- **Q3 Year 2:** Pilot projects in 10 schools, with virtual "Shark Tank" events.
- **Q4 Year 2:** Offer financial literacy workshops using free Junior Achievement resources.
- **Q1 Year 3:** Scale to all GFSC schools, with global entrepreneur mentorship.

Resource Sharing: Entrepreneurial project guides on GFSC platform. **Inclusivity:** Tailor projects to local economic contexts and languages.

Specimen Lesson Plan

Lesson: Pitching a School Start-Up Idea

Objective: Students pitch a "start-up" idea to solve a school issue.
Grade Level: 7–12
Materials: GFSC entrepreneurial template, Junior Achievement resources, paper.

Activities:

- (10 min) Introduce GFSC template; discuss entrepreneurial traits (e.g., resilience, problem-solving).
- (25 min) Groups: Develop a pitch for a school improvement idea (e.g., app for scheduling, sustainable cafeteria initiative, peer tutoring platform).
- (15 min) Groups present pitches in a "Shark Tank" format, receiving feedback from peers or invited guests.
- (10 min) Reflection: Students write about how risk-taking and innovation drive progress in the real world.

Assessment: Evaluate pitches for creativity and feasibility; review reflections.
Inclusivity: Adapt projects to local contexts; translate resources.

Chapter 19 Interdisciplinary

19. Interdisciplinary Learning: Breaking Down Subject Silos

Key Ideas: Reflecting Real-World Complexity

Interdisciplinary curricula transform global education by reflecting real-world complexity, fostering critical thinking through shared, inclusive thematic units.

- **Thematic Units Combining Subjects:** Weave together history, science, and literature around a central topic (e.g., climate change, ancient civilizations). Fosters critical thinking and creativity.
- **Cross-Disciplinary Teacher Collaboration:** Educators from different subjects work together to design integrated lessons. Enhances curriculum coherence and professional growth.
- **Student-Driven Questions:** Students propose interdisciplinary research questions (e.g., "How can we reduce urban pollution?"). Empowers them to guide learning, fostering curiosity and ownership.

Actionable Strategies: Integrating Knowledge

- **Design a Unit on Climate Change:** Combine science (data analysis), history (policy), and English (persuasive writing). *Cost: ~$200 for classroom computer. Timeline: 4-6 week unit, ongoing.*
- **Schedule Regular Teacher Planning Sessions:** Monthly 1-hour sessions for cross-disciplinary teams (e.g., science, history, English teachers) to design units. *Cost: Minimal (reallocate PD time). Timeline: Monthly, ongoing.*

- **Allow Students to Propose Interdisciplinary Research Questions:** Implement GFSC-guided inquiry projects where students propose one research question per semester. *Cost: Minimal. Timeline: 1-2 projects per semester.*
- **Create Thematic Showcases:** Host GFSC-guided events where students present unit projects (e.g., climate solution models). *Metric: 25% increase in student critical thinking.*

This chapter advocates for interdisciplinary curricula that integrate subjects like science, history, and English to mirror real-world complexity. It proposes dedicating 25% of GFSSC curricula to thematic units, such as sustainable cities, and allowing student-driven research questions. Strategies include cross-disciplinary teacher collaboration, using GFSSC templates for projects, and training teachers via webinars to align subjects. A specimen lesson plan guides students to explore topics through multiple disciplines, fostering critical thinking. The approach ensures accessibility with offline resources, supporting diverse learners, including those in low-tech settings. By aligning with 2025's focus on interconnected learning, it prepares students for complex global challenges. The broader impact is an education system that fosters holistic problem-solving, promoting equity and innovation. The GFSSC's role in sharing scalable frameworks ensures global adoption, creating inclusive, interdisciplinary environments that uplift humanity through integrated knowledge and critical thinking.

Broader Impact on Humanity and Well-Being

These key ideas transform education by fostering interdisciplinary learning. Thematic units provide holistic perspectives, preparing students for complex issues. Cross-disciplinary teacher collaboration ensures cohesive, relevant curricula. Student-driven questions foster agency and curiosity, empowering students to contribute to their communities.

Policy Highlight

Require 25% of GFSC curricula to be interdisciplinary.

- Develop thematic units combining subjects (e.g., climate change across science and history).
- Schedule teacher collaboration time for unit planning.
- Encourage student-driven interdisciplinary questions.

Implementation Plan (9 months):

- **Q2 Year 2:** Develop thematic unit templates (e.g., climate change).
- **Q3 Year 2:** Pilot units in 10 schools, with teacher collaboration time allocated.
- **Q4 Year 2:** Train teachers via GFSC webinars on interdisciplinary planning.
- **Q1 Year 3:** Scale to all GFSC schools, with student-driven questions encouraged.

Resource Sharing: Interdisciplinary unit plans on GFSC platform. **Inclusivity:** Include diverse perspectives in thematic units.

Specimen Lesson Plan

Lesson: Exploring a Topic through Multiple Subjects

Objective: Students explore a topic through multiple subjects.
Grade Level: 5–12
Materials: GFSC thematic unit template, internet access, paper.

Activities:

- (10 min) Introduce a theme (e.g., climate change, global pandemics, sustainable cities) using GFSC template.
- (25 min) Groups: Create a project combining science, history, and English (e.g., climate policy report, historical fiction piece on a pandemic, urban planning proposal).
- (15 min) Groups present projects to class; discuss interdisciplinary connections and challenges.
- (10 min) Reflection: Students write about why interdisciplinary learning is useful for understanding complex real-world issues.

Assessment: Evaluate projects for integration; assess reflections.
Inclusivity: Include diverse perspectives; translate templates.

Chapter 20 EdTech Ethics

20. Technology as a Tool, Not a Master: Ethical Integration of EdTech

Key Ideas: Ethical EdTech Integration

Balancing technology use transforms global education by enhancing learning without over-reliance, using shared open-source tools to ensure affordability and ethical implementation.

- **Balanced Screen Time:** Limit screen time with hands-on activities, ensuring technology enhances learning without overshadowing interpersonal interaction or physical engagement.
- **Ethical Discussions about Technology's Impact:** Incorporate debates on social media privacy, algorithmic bias, or digital addiction. Fosters responsible digital citizenship.
- **Open-Source Tools:** Reduce EdTech costs, making technology accessible to resource-constrained schools while maintaining quality (e.g., Moodle for course management, OpenEd for resources).

Actionable Strategies: Responsible Tech Use

- **Limit Screen Time to 50% of Class Activities:** Implement GFSC-guided schedules, capping screen-based activities and balancing with group discussions or projects. *Cost: Minimal. Timeline: Pilot in 1 grade within 3 months.*

- **Include Ethics Debates in Tech Classes:** Use GFSC-guided ethics debates with case studies (e.g., social media data breaches). *Cost: Minimal. Timeline: Monthly, ongoing.*
- **Use Free Tools Like Moodle or OpenEd:** Implement GFSC-guided open-source tools for course management and resources. *Cost: ~$200 for classroom computer. Timeline: Pilot in 1 grade within 3 months.*
- **Develop Activity Rotation Plans:** Use GFSC templates to create weekly schedules alternating digital and hands-on tasks. *Metric: 15% reduction in digital fatigue.*

This chapter emphasizes the ethical integration of educational technology (EdTech) to enhance learning while prioritizing human values. It proposes limiting screen time to 50% of instruction, using open-source tools to reduce costs, and including ethics debates on topics like social media privacy. Strategies include enforcing GFSSC guidelines for balanced tech use, developing offline activity plans, and training teachers to integrate EdTech ethically. A specimen lesson plan guides students to debate ethical tech use, fostering critical awareness. The approach aligns with 2025's focus on equitable technology, ensuring accessibility for low-resource schools through low-bandwidth solutions. By promoting affordability and privacy, it empowers schools to redirect funds to student support. The broader impact is an education system that fosters human-centered, equitable technology use, preparing students for a digital world. The GFSSC's role in providing free, ethical tools ensures global scalability, creating a connected, thoughtful society where technology serves pedagogical goals and enhances social responsibility.

Broader Impact on Humanity and Well-Being

These key ideas transform education by integrating technology ethically. Balanced screen time fosters holistic development. Ethical discussions empower students to navigate technology responsibly. Open-source tools democratize access, enabling resource-constrained schools to deliver quality education.

Policy Highlight

Enforce GFSC guidelines for balanced technology use.

- Limit screen time to 50% of instructional activities.
- Teach tech ethics using GFSC-provided case studies.
- Promote open-source tools to reduce costs.

Implementation Plan (9 months):

- **Q2 Year 2:** Develop tech ethics guidelines.
- **Q3 Year 2:** Pilot balanced tech use (50% screen time) in 10 schools.
- **Q4 Year 2:** Train teachers via GFSC webinars on ethical tech integration.
- **Q1 Year 3:** Scale to all GFSC schools, promoting open-source tools.

Resource Sharing: Ethical tech guidelines and toolkits on GFSC platform. **Inclusivity:** Tools accessible on low-cost devices and offline.

Specimen Lesson Plan

Lesson: Debating Ethical Tech Use

Objective: Students debate the ethical use of technology in learning.
Grade Level: 7–12
Materials: GFSC tech ethics guidelines, case studies, paper.

Activities:

- (10 min) Discuss GFSC guidelines; present a tech ethics case study (e.g., social media privacy, AI bias in algorithms).
- (25 min) Groups: Debate pros and cons of a specific tech tool (e.g., AI grading, personalized learning algorithms).
- (15 min) Share debate points; class votes on the most compelling arguments.
- (10 min) Reflection: Students write about how technology can be used ethically and responsibly in their daily lives.

Assessment: Evaluate debate participation; review reflections.
Inclusivity: Translate case studies; allow non-verbal debate formats.

Chapter 21 Parental Involvement

21. Parental Involvement: Redefining Family-School Partnerships

Key Ideas: Empowering Families as Partners

Engaging parents as partners transforms global education by strengthening family-school collaboration, fostering inclusive, supportive learning communities.

- **Transparent Communication:** Via digital apps (e.g., ClassDojo) or printed newsletters. Keeps parents informed about student progress, school events, and educational goals, fostering trust.
- **Parent Workshops on Supporting Learning at Home:** Equip families with tools on digital literacy, social-emotional learning, or homework strategies. GFSC provides free workshop guides and multilingual handouts.
- **Family Input in School Decision-Making:** Involving families through advisory councils ensures community voices shape policies (e.g., curriculum choices, extracurricular programs). Fosters inclusivity and ownership.

Actionable Strategies: Building Strong Partnerships

- **Use Apps like ClassDojo for Real-Time Updates:** Teachers send weekly updates on assignments, behavior, or achievements. *Cost: Minimal. Timeline: Pilot in 1 grade within 3 months.*

- **Host Monthly Parent Education Nights:** Cover topics like using educational apps or fostering SEL at home. Held in school spaces or via Zoom. *Cost: Minimal. Timeline: Monthly, ongoing.*
- **Create a Parent Advisory Council:** Establish a GFSC-guided council with diverse members, meeting quarterly to review policies. *Cost: Minimal. Timeline: Pilot in 1 grade/issue within 6 months.*
- **Create Communication Schedules:** Use GFSC templates to establish weekly update routines, alternating apps and newsletters. *Metric: 20% increase in parental involvement.*

This chapter redefines parents as active partners in education, fostering collaboration through communication schedules, workshops, and advisory councils. It proposes using free apps like ClassDojo for updates, hosting monthly parent education nights on topics like digital literacy, and conducting community surveys for feedback. Strategies include mandating parental engagement in GFSSC schools, translating materials for diverse families, and ensuring accessibility with offline options. A specimen lesson plan guides students to plan parent engagement activities, promoting shared responsibility. The approach aligns with 2025's focus on family-driven education, ensuring inclusivity for non-English speakers and low-income families. By strengthening family-school ties, it enhances student support and community involvement. The broader impact is an education system that uplifts humanity through collaborative partnerships, fostering student success and social cohesion. The GFSSC's role in sharing resources and facilitating communication ensures global scalability, creating inclusive environments where families actively contribute to educational transformation.

Broader Impact on Humanity and Well-Being

These key ideas transform schools into collaborative hubs, strengthening family-school partnerships. Transparent communication ensures all families are informed and engaged. Parent workshops empower families to support learning at home. Family input in decision-making amplifies diverse voices, ensuring schools reflect community needs.

Policy Highlight

Mandate GFSC schools to engage parents as partners.

- Use free apps like ClassDojo for parent communication.
- Host monthly parent education nights on learning support.
- Form parent advisory councils for school decisions.

Implementation Plan (9 months):

- **Q2 Year 2:** Adopt free apps like ClassDojo for parent communication.
- **Q3 Year 2:** Pilot monthly parent education nights in 10 schools.
- **Q4 Year 2:** Form parent advisory councils in pilot schools, with GFSC templates.
- **Q1 Year 3:** Scale to all GFSC schools, with translated materials.

Resource Sharing: Parent engagement guides on GFSC platform. **Inclusivity:** Translate communication materials for diverse families.

Specimen Lesson Plan

Lesson: Engaging Parents in School Activities

Objective: Students create a plan to engage parents in school activities.
Grade Level: 6–12
Materials: GFSC parent engagement guide, ClassDojo access, paper.

Activities:

- (10 min) Introduce GFSC guide; discuss various roles parents can play in school (e.g., volunteers, decision-makers, learning supporters).
- (25 min) Groups: Plan a parent education night (e.g., digital literacy workshop, SEL strategies, curriculum overview).
- (15 min) Groups present plans to class, detailing how they will attract and engage diverse families.
- (10 min) Reflection: Students write about why parent involvement is important for student success and a strong school community.

Assessment: Evaluate plans for feasibility and inclusivity; assess reflections.
Inclusivity: Translate plans for diverse families; offer virtual options.

22. Global Learning Networks: Connecting Classrooms Worldwide

Key Ideas: Fostering Global Perspectives

Connecting classrooms globally transforms education by enabling cross-cultural collaboration, fostering inclusive, global perspectives at minimal cost.

- **Virtual Pen Pal Programs:** Connect students with peers in other countries (e.g., ePals) to exchange messages, videos, or cultural artifacts. Builds cross-cultural communication skills and reduces stereotypes.
- **Joint Projects with International Schools:** Students collaborate on shared goals (e.g., digital magazine, sustainability campaign), blending diverse perspectives and skills. Develops teamwork, digital literacy, and problem-solving.
- **Global Issue Discussions via Video Conferencing:** Connect students worldwide to debate and explore topics like climate change, peace, or inequality (e.g., Zoom). Fosters critical thinking and global awareness.

Actionable Strategies: Building a Connected World

- **Join Platforms like ePals:** Implement GFSC-guided ePals programs, pairing students with international peers for monthly exchanges. *Cost: Minimal. Timeline: Pilot in 1 class within 3 months.*

- **Assign Joint Projects with Overseas Schools:** Pair classes to create a digital magazine on topics like climate solutions, collaborating via Google Docs. *Cost: ~$100 for shared tablet. Timeline: 1-2 projects per semester.*
- **Use Zoom for Monthly Global Discussion Forums:** Connect classes with international peers to discuss issues like climate resilience. *Cost: ~$200 for webcam. Timeline: Monthly, ongoing.*
- **Create Cultural Exchange Galleries:** Develop GFSC-supported digital or physical displays of pen pal artifacts, like drawings, shared via ePals or school boards. *Metric: 20% increase in student global competence.*

This chapter emphasizes global learning networks to connect classrooms worldwide, fostering cross-cultural understanding and collaboration. It proposes using platforms like PenPal Schools for virtual exchanges, creating cultural exchange galleries, and developing global project portfolios. Strategies include mandating GFSSC schools to join networks, facilitating joint projects on issues like climate change, and ensuring offline options for accessibility. A specimen lesson plan guides students to collaborate with global peers, promoting empathy and cultural competence. The approach aligns with 2025's sustainability and peace goals, supporting diverse learners through multilingual resources. By connecting students across borders, it breaks cultural barriers and fosters global citizenship. The broader impact is an education system that promotes peace and cooperation, preparing students for interconnected challenges. The GFSSC's role in providing scalable platforms and resources ensures accessibility, creating a world where students collaborate globally to drive innovation and empathy.

Broader Impact on Humanity and Well-Being

These key ideas transform education by harnessing global learning networks. Virtual pen pal programs cultivate global empathy. Joint projects build collaboration skills and promote innovation. Global issue discussions foster critical thinking and empathy, preparing students to address interconnected challenges.

Policy Highlight

Require GFSC schools to participate in global exchange programs.

- Facilitate virtual exchanges via GFSC partnerships with platforms like ePals.
- Integrate UN Sustainable Development Goals into curricula.
- Offer multilingual resources for global issue discussions.

Implementation Plan (10 months):

- **Q2 Year 2:** Partner with platforms like ePals for virtual exchanges.
- **Q3 Year 2:** Develop curricula on UN Sustainable Development Goals, shared freely via GFSC.
- **Q4 Year 2:** Pilot exchanges in 10 schools, with feedback shared globally.
- **Q1 Year 3:** Scale exchanges to all GFSC schools, with GFSC subsidies for internet access.

Resource Sharing: Exchange templates and curricula on GFSC platform. **Inclusivity:** Multilingual resources, offline exchange options (e.g., letter-writing).

Specimen Lesson Plan

Lesson: Collaborating on a Global Issue

Objective: Students collaborate with a global partner school on a shared issue.
Grade Level: 5–12
Materials: GFSC exchange platform (e.g., ePals), UN SDG resources, Google Docs.

Activities:

- (10 min) Introduce UN SDGs; show GFSC exchange platform.
- (25 min) Pairs: Draft a collaborative project plan with a partner school (e.g., water conservation, cultural preservation, sustainable energy).
- (15 min) Share plans; discuss cultural insights gained and challenges of global collaboration.
- (10 min) Reflection: Students write about how global collaboration helps solve complex problems and builds understanding.

Assessment: Evaluate plans for clarity; review reflections for global awareness.
Inclusivity: Provide offline exchange options; translate resources.

Chapter 23 Flexible Scheduling

23. Flexible Scheduling: Reimagining the School Day and Year

Key Ideas: Optimizing Engagement and Outcomes

Reimagining the school day and year with flexible scheduling transforms education by optimizing student engagement, catering to individual learning rhythms, and supporting holistic well-being.

- **Block Scheduling:** Longer blocks for deep, project-based work, shorter sessions for targeted skill instruction. Allows for more varied activities and interdisciplinary work.
- **Year-Round Schooling with Shorter Breaks:** More frequent, shorter breaks throughout the year instead of a long summer break. Reduces learning loss and maintains engagement.
- **Student Choice in Daily Schedules:** Older students design their daily schedules within set parameters, choosing electives or prioritizing project time. Fosters autonomy and aligns education with individual needs.

Actionable Strategies: Designing Responsive Environments

- **Pilot Block Scheduling for Core Subjects:** Implement 90-minute blocks for math and English, allowing for deeper dives and varied activities. *Timeline: Pilot in 1* *grade within 6 months.*

- **Transition to a Balanced Calendar:** Shift to a year-round schedule with 4-week breaks every 10 weeks. Communicate changes to parents using GFSC templates. *Timeline: Pilot in 1 grade within 1 year.*
- **Allow Older Students to Design Their Schedules:** For grades 9-12, allow selection of 1-2 daily periods (e.g., electives, project blocks) within a framework ensuring core subject coverage. *Cost: Minimal. Timeline: Pilot in 1 grade within 6 months.*
- **Offer Break Enrichment Programs:** Develop GFSC-supported mini-camps during breaks, focusing on skills like robotics. *Metric: 15% increase in student engagement.*

This chapter reimagines school schedules to optimize engagement through block scheduling, year-round schooling, and student choice in daily schedules. It proposes piloting block scheduling for deeper learning, transitioning to shorter breaks, and allowing older students to design schedules within parameters. Strategies include using GFSSC templates for scheduling, training teachers via webinars, and ensuring accessibility with offline guides. A specimen lesson plan guides students to propose flexible schedules, fostering autonomy. The approach aligns with 2025's focus on continuous learning, addressing gaps for underserved students. By accommodating diverse needs, it enhances engagement and career alignment. The broader impact is an education system that supports personalized learning and equity, preparing students for dynamic futures. The GFSSC's role in sharing scalable frameworks ensures global adoption, creating flexible, inclusive schools that uplift humanity through tailored educational experiences.

Broader Impact on Humanity and Well-Being

These key ideas transform education by creating more dynamic, responsive, and effective learning environments. Block scheduling allows for deeper engagement. Year-round schooling reduces learning loss. Student choice promotes self-regulation and prepares students for independent decision-making, enhancing personal growth and global workforce readiness.

Policy Highlight

Mandate flexible scheduling models in GFSC schools.

- Implement block scheduling for core subjects.
- Pilot year-round schooling with shorter, more frequent breaks.
- Allow student choice in daily schedules for older students.

Implementation Plan (12 months):

- **Q2 Year 2:** Develop GFSC flexible scheduling frameworks.
- **Q3 Year 2:** Pilot block scheduling in 10 schools.
- **Q4 Year 2:** Pilot year-round schooling in 5 schools.
- **Q1 Year 3:** Scale to all GFSC schools, with student choice options.

Resource Sharing: Scheduling templates and case studies on GFSC platform. **Inclusivity:** Adapt models for diverse student needs and contexts.

Specimen Lesson Plan

Lesson: Designing an Ideal Flexible School Schedule

Objective: Students design an ideal flexible school schedule for their grade level.
Grade Level: 7–12
Materials: GFSC flexible scheduling templates, school calendar, colored pens.

Activities:

- (10 min) Introduce concepts of block scheduling and year-round schooling using GFSC templates.
- (25 min) Small groups: Design a proposed daily and yearly schedule for their grade, including time for core subjects, projects, and breaks.
- (15 min) Groups present their schedules, explaining the benefits and challenges of their design.
- (10 min) Reflection: Students write about how flexible scheduling could improve their learning experience and well-being.

Assessment: Evaluate schedules for creativity and practicality; assess reflections.
Inclusivity: Consider diverse student needs (e.g., extracurriculars, part-time jobs) in design proposals.

Chapter 24 Career Readiness

24. Career Readiness: Bridging School and the Future Workforce

Key Ideas: Preparing for a Dynamic Workforce

Bridging school and the future workforce transforms global education by equipping students with practical skills and real-world experiences, ensuring adaptability and employability.

- **Internship and Apprenticeship Programs:** Provide hands-on experience in various industries. Students gain practical skills, network with professionals, and explore career paths.
- **Soft Skills Development:** Workshops and activities focused on communication, collaboration, critical thinking, and adaptability. Essential for success in any modern workplace.
- **Career Mentorship and Counseling:** Connect students with professionals for guidance and support. Helps students identify interests, set career goals, and navigate educational pathways.

Actionable Strategies: Building Future-Ready Skills

- **Establish a School-Wide Internship Program:** Partner with local businesses and organizations to offer short-term internships (e.g., 2-4 weeks) for high school students. *Timeline: Pilot with 5-10 businesses within 6 months.*
- **Integrate Soft Skills Workshops into Advisory Periods:** Dedicate weekly sessions to activities focusing on communication, problem-solving, and teamwork using GFSC

modules. *Cost: Minimal. Timeline: Weekly, ongoing.*

- **Launch a Career Mentorship Network:** Connect students with alumni and local professionals via virtual platforms (e.g., LinkedIn for Education, Zoom). *Timeline: Pilot with 10 mentors within 3 months.*
- **Host Annual Career Fairs:** Invite diverse professionals to speak about their fields and offer hands-on activities. *Metric: 15% increase in student self-reported career clarity.*

This chapter focuses on preparing students for future economies through career exploration electives, internships, and soft skills training like teamwork and communication. It proposes partnering with businesses for job shadowing, integrating soft skills into group projects, and using GFSSC career curricula. Strategies include mandating career readiness programs in GFSSC schools, ensuring opportunities for underrepresented groups, and providing offline resources for accessibility. A specimen lesson plan guides students to explore career paths through research and role-play, fostering practical skills. The approach aligns with 2025's workforce demands in tech and healthcare, ensuring inclusivity for diverse learners. By bridging school and work, it prepares students for economic volatility. The broader impact is an education system that fosters equitable access to opportunities, empowering students for successful careers. The GFSSC's role in facilitating partnerships and sharing resources ensures scalability, creating a world where students thrive in dynamic, inclusive economies.

Broader Impact on Humanity and Well-Being

These key ideas transform education by directly preparing students for the future workforce. Internships and apprenticeships provide invaluable practical experience. Soft skills development ensures adaptability and effective collaboration. Career mentorship and counseling empower students to make informed decisions, reducing unemployment and fostering economic stability.

Policy Highlight

Mandate career readiness programs in GFSC schools.

- Implement internship and apprenticeship programs with local businesses.
- Integrate soft skills development into curricula.
- Establish career mentorship and counseling services.

Implementation Plan (12 months):

- **Q2 Year 2:** Develop GFSC career readiness framework with internship templates.
- **Q3 Year 2:** Pilot internship programs in 10 schools with local business partners.
- **Q4 Year 2:** Train teachers on soft skills integration via GFSC webinars.
- **Q1 Year 3:** Scale to all GFSC schools, with career mentorship networks established.

Resource Sharing: Career readiness guides and templates on GFSC platform. **Inclusivity:** Tailor programs to local economic needs and diverse student aspirations.

Specimen Lesson Plan

Lesson: Planning a Future Career Path

Objective: Students research a future career path and present a plan for acquiring necessary skills.
Grade Level: 9–12
Materials: Internet access, GFSC career readiness guide, presentation software.

Activities:

- (10 min) Introduce the concept of future workforce skills and career pathways using the GFSC guide.
- (25 min) Individual/Pairs: Research a career path of interest, identifying required academic skills, soft skills, and potential internship/mentorship opportunities.
- (15 min) Students present their findings and a personal action plan to the class.
- (10 min) Reflection: Students write about how their chosen career aligns with their passions and how they plan to develop the necessary skills.

Assessment: Evaluate research for thoroughness; assess action plans for feasibility; review reflections.
Inclusivity: Provide resources for diverse career paths; support multilingual research.

Chapter 25 Cultural Relevance

25. Cultural Relevance: Curricula That Reflect Diverse Identities

Key Ideas: Honoring Diverse Identities

The Future School emphasizes culturally relevant curricula that honor students' diverse backgrounds, fostering inclusion, engagement, and a sense of belonging.

- **Diverse Literature and Historical Perspectives:** Incorporate texts by authors from under-represented groups and examine historical events from indigenous perspectives. Validates identities and challenges stereotypes.
- **Student-Led Cultural Showcases:** Organize events where students present cultural traditions (e.g., dances, recipes, storytelling). Fosters pride, peer understanding, and community connection.
- **Teacher Training in Cultural Sensitivity:** Workshops on culturally responsive pedagogy, implicit bias, and creating inclusive classroom environments. Ensures educators can adapt instruction effectively.

Actionable Strategies: Cultivating Inclusive Curricula

- **Curate a Diverse Library:** Build a classroom library using GFSC-curated book lists, sourcing titles through community donations. Books reflect student cultures. *Cost: ~$100 for 50-100 titles. Timeline: Ongoing.*
- **Host Quarterly Cultural Showcases:** Organize student-led events where students present cultural projects (e.g., family traditions, local folklore). *Cost: Minimal. Timeline: Quarterly.*

- **Train Teachers in Culturally Responsive Pedagogy:** Use GFSC-curated training modules from organizations like Learning for Justice. *Timeline: 3-hour webinar series, ongoing.*
- **Integrate Local Histories and Traditions:** Develop lesson plans that connect global concepts to local cultural contexts, using community experts as guest speakers. *Metric: 15% boost in student self-esteem.*

This chapter champions culturally relevant curricula to honor diverse student identities, fostering inclusion and engagement. It proposes curating diverse literature, hosting student-led cultural showcases, and training teachers in cultural sensitivity using resources like the Zinn Education Project. Strategies include mandating culturally relevant curricula in GFSSC schools, creating digital cultural archives, and ensuring accessibility with offline guides. A specimen lesson plan guides students to create culturally relevant presentations, promoting pride in heritage. The approach aligns with 2025's focus on cultural equity, supporting diverse learners, including non-native speakers. By reflecting local and global cultures, it enhances belonging and academic success. The broader impact is an education system that uplifts humanity through inclusive, engaging learning experiences that celebrate diversity. The GFSSC's role in sharing scalable resources ensures global adoption, creating schools where all students feel valued and empowered to contribute to a compassionate, multicultural world.

Broader Impact on Humanity and Well-Being

These key ideas transform education by creating inclusive, equitable environments that honor diversity. Diverse curricula enhance engagement and promote equity. Student-led showcases foster cultural pride and peer understanding. Teacher training ensures educators can adapt instruction effectively, strengthening social cohesion.

Policy Highlight

Mandate culturally relevant curricula in GFSC schools.

- Integrate diverse literature and historical perspectives into lessons.
- Promote student-led cultural showcases.
- Provide teacher training in cultural sensitivity and culturally responsive pedagogy.

Implementation Plan (9 months):

- **Q2 Year 2:** Develop GFSC culturally relevant curriculum frameworks.
- **Q3 Year 2:** Pilot diverse literature and history units in 10 schools.
- **Q4 Year 2:** Train teachers via GFSC webinars on cultural sensitivity.
- **Q1 Year 3:** Scale to all GFSC schools, with student-led cultural showcases.

Resource Sharing: Culturally relevant curricula and resources on GFSC platform. **Inclusivity:** Multilingual resources, local community input.

Specimen Lesson Plan

Lesson: Exploring Cultural Traditions

Objective: Students explore a cultural tradition and present its significance to the class.
Grade Level: 4–12
Materials: GFSC cultural relevance guide, internet access (optional), art supplies.

Activities:

- (10 min) Introduce the concept of cultural relevance; discuss examples of diverse traditions using the GFSC guide.
- (25 min) Individual/Pairs: Research a cultural tradition (from their own background or another they are curious about) and prepare a presentation (e.g., a short skit, a visual art piece, a recipe demonstration).
- (15 min) Students present their chosen tradition, explaining its historical and social significance.
- (10 min) Reflection: Students write about how understanding diverse cultures enriches their learning and promotes empathy.

Assessment: Evaluate presentations for cultural insight and creativity; assess reflections.
Inclusivity: Encourage students to share their own cultural heritage; allow diverse presentation formats (e.g., verbal, visual).

Chapter 26 Data Driven

26. Data-Driven Decision Making: Using Analytics to Improve Outcomes

Key Ideas: Optimizing Learning with Data

Data-driven decision making transforms global education by using analytics to identify student strengths and areas for improvement, ensuring targeted interventions and equitable outcomes.

- **AI Analytics for Student Performance:** Provide teachers with actionable insights by analyzing data from assignments, quizzes, or platform interactions. Highlights strengths and areas for improvement.
- **Formative Assessment Data:** Frequent, low-stakes assessments (e.g., exit tickets, quick polls) provide real-time feedback to guide instruction. Allows teachers to adjust lessons immediately.
- **Equity Data Audits:** Analyze demographic data alongside academic outcomes to identify and address systemic disparities. Ensures resources and support are equitably distributed.

Actionable Strategies: Informed Decisions

- **Pilot AI Analytics Dashboards:** Use GFSC-approved tools (e.g., Edmodo dashboards) to track student progress without compromising privacy. *Cost: Minimal. Timeline: Pilot in 1 class within 3 months.*

- **Implement Weekly Formative Assessments:** Use tools like Google Forms or Socrative for quick quizzes and polls. Teachers use data to adjust lessons. *Cost: Minimal. Timeline: Weekly, ongoing.*
- **Conduct Annual Equity Data Audits:** Form a task force to analyze school-wide data (e.g., suspension rates, test scores by demographic) using GFSC audit templates. *Timeline: Annually.*
- **Share Analytics Summaries with Students and Parents:** Provide simplified, GFSC-formatted reports during check-ins, fostering transparency and motivation. *Metric: 10% improvement in student outcomes.*

This chapter promotes data-driven decision making to personalize learning and enhance outcomes while safeguarding privacy. It proposes using platforms like Edmodo for tracking, creating teacher dashboards for real-time insights, and involving students in data reflection through portfolios. Strategies include mandating ethical data use in GFSSC schools, conducting quarterly data reviews, and ensuring accessibility with offline charts. A specimen lesson plan guides students to analyze their learning data to set goals, fostering self-regulation. The approach aligns with 2025's data privacy laws, supporting diverse learners and educators. By leveraging analytics, it improves teaching effectiveness and student engagement, particularly in underserved areas. The broader impact is an equitable, responsive education system that optimizes outcomes through informed decisions. The GFSSC's role in providing secure, multilingual data tools ensures global scalability, creating a connected, efficient educational landscape that uplifts humanity through personalized, data-informed learning.

Broader Impact on Humanity and Well-Being

These key ideas transform education by making it more responsive and equitable. AI analytics empower teachers to address individual needs. Formative assessment data ensures timely interventions. Equity data audits promote fairness and reduce disparities, fostering a more just and capable global society.

Policy Highlight

Mandate data-driven decision making in GFSC schools.

- Implement AI analytics to identify student strengths and areas for improvement.
- Require regular formative assessments to guide instruction.
- Conduct annual equity data audits to ensure fair outcomes.

Implementation Plan (9 months):

- **Q2 Year 2:** Develop GFSC data analysis frameworks and privacy guidelines.
- **Q3 Year 2:** Pilot AI analytics dashboards in 10 schools.
- **Q4 Year 2:** Train teachers via GFSC webinars on using formative assessment data.
- **Q1 Year 3:** Scale to all GFSC schools, with annual equity data audits.

Resource Sharing: Data analysis tools and templates on GFSC platform. **Inclusivity:** Ensure data privacy and ethical use, provide multilingual guides.

Specimen Lesson Plan

Lesson: Analyzing Classroom Data for Learning Patterns

Objective: Students analyze classroom data to identify learning patterns and propose solutions.
Grade Level: 6–12
Materials: Sample anonymous class data (e.g., quiz scores, participation rates), GFSC data analysis template, graph paper or spreadsheet software.

Activities:

- (10 min) Introduce data-driven decision making; discuss ethical use of data using GFSC guidelines.
- (25 min) Small groups: Analyze provided anonymous class data using the GFSC template, looking for trends or areas of improvement.
- (15 min) Groups present their findings and propose strategies to improve learning outcomes based on the data.
- (10 min) Reflection: Students write about how data can help teachers personalize learning and ensure fairness.

Assessment: Evaluate data analysis for accuracy; assess proposed solutions for creativity and feasibility; review reflections.
Inclusivity: Provide data in accessible formats; support diverse analysis methods.

Chapter 27 Role of Play

27. The Role of Play: Learning Through Joy and Exploration

Key Ideas: Fostering Creativity and Engagement

Integrating play-based learning transforms global education by using games and joyful activities to teach concepts, fostering creativity, engagement, and social-emotional development.

- **Gamified Learning Experiences:** Incorporate game elements (points, badges, leaderboards) into lessons to boost motivation and engagement. Uses educational games or digital platforms.
- **Unstructured Play Time:** Dedicated periods for free, imaginative play, fostering creativity, problem-solving, and social skills. Can be indoors or outdoors, with simple materials.
- **Play-Based Curriculum Units:** Design entire units around playful exploration (e.g., building a city with blocks to learn urban planning, role-playing historical events). Integrates academic content with joyful activities.

Actionable Strategies: Embracing Joyful Learning

- **Integrate Educational Games into Lessons:** Use GFSC-curated free educational games (e.g., Prodigy for math, Kahoot! for quizzes) for 15-20 minutes weekly. *Cost: Minimal. Timeline: Weekly, ongoing.*
- **Schedule Daily Unstructured Play Time:** Dedicate 15-30 minutes daily for free play with open-ended materials (e.g., building blocks, art supplies, outdoor nature

elements). *Cost: Minimal. Timeline: Daily, ongoing.*

- **Design Play-Based Project Units:** Create units where students learn through playful construction, role-playing, or simulations (e.g., building a model ecosystem). *Timeline: 1-2 units per semester.*
- **Train Teachers on Play-Based Pedagogies:** Use GFSC webinars to equip teachers with strategies for facilitating play-based learning and integrating academic content. *Metric: 20% increase in student engagement.*

This chapter highlights play-based learning to foster creativity, problem-solving, and engagement across all ages. It proposes gamified lessons using platforms like Kahoot, daily outdoor recess with structured games, and simulations for older students to address real-world issues. Strategies include mandating daily play-based learning in GFSSC schools, creating gamified challenges, and ensuring accessibility with offline toolkits. A specimen lesson plan guides students to learn through game-based activities, enhancing retention. The approach aligns with 2025's focus on mental health and interactive learning, supporting diverse learners through inclusive activities. By fostering joy and exploration, it improves academic and social outcomes, preparing students for global challenges like sustainability. The broader impact is an education system that nurtures resilient, creative students through joyful learning experiences. The GFSSC's role in sharing scalable, low-cost resources ensures global adoption, creating inclusive environments where play drives innovation and well-being.

Broader Impact on Humanity and Well-Being

These key ideas transform education by making learning joyful, engaging, and holistic. Gamified experiences boost motivation. Unstructured play fosters creativity and social skills. Play-based curricula integrate academic content with exploration, enhancing well-being and preparing students for innovative futures.

Policy Highlight

Mandate play-based learning in GFSC schools.

- Integrate gamified learning experiences into curricula.
- Provide dedicated unstructured play time daily.
- Develop play-based curriculum units across subjects.

Implementation Plan (9 months):

- **Q2 Year 2:** Develop GFSC play-based learning framework with activity guides.
- **Q3 Year 2:** Pilot gamified lessons and unstructured play in 10 schools.
- **Q4 Year 2:** Train teachers via GFSC webinars on play-based pedagogies.
- **Q1 Year 3:** Scale to all GFSC schools, with play-based curriculum units.

Resource Sharing: Play-based learning guides and game lists on GFSC platform. **Inclusivity:** Adapt activities for diverse ages and abilities, provide multilingual resources.

Specimen Lesson Plan

Lesson: Learning History Through Role-Playing

Objective: Students learn about historical events through role-playing a significant moment.
Grade Level: 4–8
Materials: GFSC play-based learning guide, historical event brief, simple props (optional).

Activities:

- (10 min) Introduce a historical event (e.g., a key moment in a civil rights movement, a scientific discovery) using the GFSC guide.
- (25 min) Small groups: Assign roles to students and have them role-play the historical event, focusing on the perspectives and emotions of the characters.
- (15 min) Groups present their role-plays; class discusses the historical context and lessons learned.
- (10 min) Reflection: Students write about what they learned about the event and the people involved through play.

Assessment: Observe participation in role-play; assess reflections for historical understanding and empathy.
Inclusivity: Adapt roles for diverse abilities; allow non-verbal forms of expression.

Chapter 28 Restorative Practices

28. Restorative Practices: Building Positive School Cultures

Key Ideas: Fostering Accountability and Community

Restorative practices transform global education by prioritizing accountability and community over punitive discipline, building positive, inclusive school cultures.

- **Restorative Circles:** Structured discussions to address conflicts, build relationships, and foster empathy. All parties involved have a voice in repairing harm.
- **Proactive Relationship Building:** Activities that foster positive connections among students and staff (e.g., team-building games, community-building circles). Prevents conflicts before they escalate.
- **Student Leadership in Conflict Resolution:** Train students to mediate peer conflicts and facilitate restorative conversations. Empowers students to take ownership of their school community.

Actionable Strategies: Cultivating Positive Cultures

- **Implement Weekly Restorative Circles:** Dedicate 15-20 minutes weekly for circles to discuss class norms, resolve minor conflicts, or build community. Use GFSC circle guides. *Cost: Minimal. Timeline: Weekly, ongoing.*
- **Train Staff in Restorative Practices:** Provide GFSC webinars on restorative dialogue, conflict resolution, and relationship building. *Timeline: 2-hour webinar, ongoing.*

- **Establish a Peer Mediation Program:** Train students to mediate conflicts among peers using GFSC mediation templates. *Cost: Minimal. Timeline: Pilot with 10 students within 6 months.*
- **Integrate Restorative Language:** Encourage staff and students to use "I" statements and focus on impact (e.g., "How did that make you feel?"). *Metric: 30% reduction in disciplinary referrals.*

This chapter advocates replacing punitive discipline with restorative practices like circles and peer mediation to foster positive, inclusive school cultures. It proposes training staff and students in restorative principles, hosting mediation showcases, and using GFSSC templates for accessibility. Strategies include mandating restorative practices in GFSSC schools, implementing weekly circles to discuss dynamics, and ensuring cultural diversity in training. A specimen lesson plan guides students to resolve conflicts using restorative circles, promoting empathy. The approach aligns with 2025's restorative justice trends, supporting diverse learners, including those with language barriers. By prioritizing accountability and community, it reduces inequities in discipline and enhances social well-being. The broader impact is an education system that fosters empathetic, resilient communities through inclusive practices. The GFSSC's role in sharing free resources ensures global scalability, creating harmonious schools that uplift humanity through restorative justice and equity.

Broader Impact on Humanity and Well-Being

These key ideas transform education by building positive, inclusive school cultures. Restorative circles address conflicts constructively. Proactive relationship building prevents issues. Student leadership in conflict resolution empowers students, fostering empathy and social cohesion.

Policy Highlight

Replace punitive discipline with restorative practices in GFSC schools.

- Implement restorative circles for conflict resolution and community building.
- Provide staff training on restorative practices.
- Establish student leadership programs for conflict mediation.

Implementation Plan (9 months):

- **Q2 Year 2:** Develop GFSC restorative practice framework with circle guides.
- **Q3 Year 2:** Train staff via GFSC webinars on restorative dialogue.
- **Q4 Year 2:** Pilot restorative circles and peer mediation in 10 schools.
- **Q1 Year 3:** Scale to all GFSC schools, with student leadership programs.

Resource Sharing: Restorative practice guides and training modules on GFSC platform.
Inclusivity: Adapt practices for diverse cultural contexts and student needs.

Specimen Lesson Plan

Lesson: Participating in a Restorative Circle

Objective: Students participate in a restorative circle to address a hypothetical classroom conflict.
Grade Level: 5–12
Materials: GFSC restorative circle guide, talking piece (e.g., a soft ball), scenario card.

Activities:

- (10 min) Introduce restorative circles and their purpose using the GFSC guide; explain roles (facilitator, participants).
- (25 min) Students participate in a simulated restorative circle for a hypothetical classroom conflict (e.g., a group project disagreement, a misunderstanding).
- (15 min) Discuss the process: What was challenging? What was effective? How was harm addressed?
- (10 min) Reflection: Students write about how restorative practices can build a more positive and fair school community.

Assessment: Observe participation in the circle; assess reflections for understanding of restorative principles.
Inclusivity: Ensure all voices are heard; provide opportunities for non-verbal participation.

Chapter 29 Teacher PD

29. Teacher Professional Development: Lifelong Growth for Educators

Key Ideas: Empowering Educators for Continuous Growth

Investing in the lifelong growth of educators transforms global education by empowering teachers with innovative skills, cutting-edge knowledge, and a renewed sense of purpose.

- **Peer-Led Learning Communities (PLCs):** Teachers regularly engage in collaborative learning, sharing best practices, and co-developing innovative strategies. Fosters a culture of continuous improvement.
- **Access to Free Online Courses:** Provides educators with flexible, self-paced learning opportunities on new pedagogies, EdTech, or subject-specific content (e.g., Coursera for Teachers, edX). GFSC partnerships curate vetted courses.
- **Time for Collaborative Planning and Innovation:** Dedicated time for teachers to co-design interdisciplinary units, innovate teaching strategies, and align curricula with student needs. Reduces isolation and fosters creativity.

Actionable Strategies: Supporting Teacher Growth

- **Form Peer-Led Learning Communities:** Establish GFSC-guided PLCs in each school, meeting weekly or bi-weekly to discuss pedagogical challenges and share solutions.

Cost: Minimal. Timeline: Weekly/Bi-weekly, ongoing.

- **Provide Access to Free Online Courses:** Curate free courses from platforms like Coursera or edX. Teachers complete one self-directed course per semester. *Cost: Minimal. Timeline: 1 course per semester, ongoing.*
- **Allocate One Day per Month for Co-Planning:** Dedicate 6 hours monthly for teachers to co-design interdisciplinary units (e.g., history-science project on pandemics). *Cost: Minimal (substitute coverage). Timeline: Monthly, ongoing.*
- **Host Teacher Showcases:** Organize quarterly events where teachers present a problem they've explored or a new teaching tool, inspiring students and peers. *Metric: 20% increase in teacher professional confidence.*

This chapter emphasizes continuous professional development to keep teachers innovative and effective in evolving classrooms. It proposes forming peer-led learning communities, providing access to free online courses like Coursera, and allocating monthly planning days for interdisciplinary units. Strategies include mandating professional development in GFSSC schools, creating course cohorts, and ensuring accessibility with offline agendas. A specimen lesson plan guides students to simulate professional development sessions, fostering collaboration. The approach aligns with 2025's demand for teacher-led innovation, addressing local challenges like student engagement. By empowering educators with new skills, it enhances teaching quality and student outcomes. The broader impact is an education system that uplifts humanity through adaptive, creative teaching practices. The GFSSC's role in sharing scalable, multilingual resources ensures global adoption, creating vibrant learning environments where educators thrive and inspire diverse learners to succeed.

Broader Impact on Humanity and Well-Being

These key ideas transform education by fostering continuous professional development for teachers. Peer-led learning communities enhance collaboration. Access to online courses provides flexible learning. Dedicated planning time fosters innovation, ensuring educators remain effective and inspired, leading to better student outcomes.

Policy Highlight

Mandate continuous professional development for GFSC teachers.

- Form peer-led learning communities in each school.
- Provide access to free online courses via GFSC partnerships.
- Allocate monthly planning days for innovation.

Implementation Plan (9 months):

- **Q2 Year 2:** Form peer-led learning communities, with GFSC templates.
- **Q3 Year 2:** Provide access to free courses via GFSC partnerships with Coursera.
- **Q4 Year 2:** Pilot monthly planning days in 10 schools.
- **Q1 Year 3:** Scale to all GFSC schools, with multilingual PD options.

Resource Sharing: PD modules and videos on GFSC platform. **Inclusivity:** Offer PD in multiple languages and formats.

Specimen Lesson Plan

Lesson: Simulating Teacher Professional Development

Objective: Students simulate a professional development session for teachers.
Grade Level: 8–12
Materials: GFSC PD module (sample), topic list (e.g., inquiry-based learning, formative assessment), paper.

Activities:

- (10 min) Introduce the concept of teacher professional development using a GFSC module; discuss why continuous growth is important for educators.
- (25 min) Groups: Plan and deliver a 5-minute professional development session on a specific teaching strategy (e.g., how to implement a growth mindset in class, using a new digital tool).
- (15 min) Groups present their sessions to class, acting as "teachers" training their "peers."
- (10 min) Reflection: Students write about why teacher learning is important for creating a dynamic and effective school environment.

Assessment: Evaluate sessions for clarity and engagement; review reflections.
Inclusivity: Translate modules; allow diverse presentation formats.

Chapter 30 Future Ecosystem

30. The Future School Ecosystem: Scaling Transformation Globally

Key Ideas: Building a Global Network

Scaling a global consortium transforms education by uniting schools in a shared, inclusive ecosystem, leveraging open resources to make innovative, equitable education universally accessible.

- **Policy Advocacy for Innovative Models:** Strategic engagement with governments and policymakers to secure systemic support for flexible, inclusive education. GFSC provides policy briefs and lobbying guides.
- **Global Partnerships to Share Best Practices:** Collaboration with international organizations (e.g., UNESCO, NGOs) to exchange effective pedagogies, curricula, and tools. Accelerates innovation and promotes cross-cultural learning.
- **Scalable Frameworks for Resource-Constrained Schools:** Develop "Future School Toolkits" with free, adaptable resources (e.g., offline learning kits, low-cost tech blueprints). Ensures equitable access to transformative models globally.

Actionable Strategies: Scaling Global Transformation

- **Advocate for Flexible Curriculum Standards:** Engage with local school boards and education ministries using GFSC policy briefs to promote competency-based learning. *Timeline: Ongoing lobbying efforts.*
- **Join Global Education Networks:** Connect with organizations like UNESCO's ASPnet to exchange ideas, participate in joint research, and share best practices. *Timeline:*

Ongoing partnerships.

- **Develop a "Future School Toolkit":** Create a comprehensive toolkit with free resources (e.g., lesson plans, design guides, policy templates) for schools worldwide. *Cost: Minimal. Timeline: Q2 Year 2.*
- **Host Virtual Global Summits:** Organize annual summits via Zoom to draft GFSC charters, share vision statements, and foster international collaboration. *Metric: 15% increase in GFSC member schools annually.*

This chapter envisions a global ecosystem for scaling the Future School model through the GFSSC, rooted in innovation, equity, and student-centered learning. It proposes policy advocacy for flexible curricula, partnerships with networks like UNESCO's ASPnet, and developing a free "Future School Toolkit" for resource-constrained schools. Strategies include forming advocacy coalitions, hosting virtual exchange fairs, and establishing toolkit hubs for local training. A specimen lesson plan guides students to propose GFSC initiatives, fostering global awareness. The approach aligns with 2025's equity and sustainability goals, ensuring inclusivity for rural and low-income schools through offline resources. By scaling best practices globally, it creates a cohesive, innovative education system that addresses local needs while fostering cross-cultural collaboration. The broader impact is a transformative global education network that uplifts humanity through accessible, equitable learning. The GFSSC's role in sharing resources and facilitating partnerships ensures scalability, creating a world where every child thrives in a future-ready school.

Broader Impact on Humanity and Well-Being

These key ideas create a global ecosystem for scaling the future school model. Policy advocacy secures systemic support, enabling flexible, inclusive education. Global partnerships share best practices, accelerating innovation. Scalable frameworks ensure resource-constrained schools access future-ready models, democratizing education and reducing inequities.

Policy Highlight

Establish a GFSC framework for global scaling.

- Advocate for flexible education policies via GFSC lobbying.
- Partner with UNESCO and other networks to share best practices.
- Develop a free "Future School Toolkit" for all schools.

Implementation Plan (12 months):

- **Q2 Year 2:** Develop a "Future School Toolkit," shared on the GFSC platform.
- **Q3 Year 2:** Partner with UNESCO to share best practices globally.
- **Q4 Year 2:** Advocate for flexible policies at regional education conferences.
- **Q1 Year 3:** Scale the GFSC framework to 100 schools, with ongoing support.

Resource Sharing: All resources on an open-access GFSC platform. **Inclusivity:** Resources tailored for low-resource and diverse contexts.

Specimen Lesson Plan

Lesson: Proposing a Global GFSC Initiative

Objective: Students propose a GFSC initiative for global scaling.
Grade Level: 7–12
Materials: GFSC toolkit, UNESCO resources, Google Docs.

Activities:

- (10 min) Introduce GFSC toolkit; discuss global education challenges and opportunities for scaling innovation.
- (25 min) Groups: Propose an initiative (e.g., global STEAM challenge, universal digital literacy program, cross-cultural mental health support network) that the GFSC could scale globally.
- (15 min) Groups present proposals to class, detailing their impact and feasibility for widespread adoption.
- (10 min) Reflection: Students write about how global collaboration can transform schools and uplift humanity on a large scale.

Assessment: Evaluate proposals for feasibility and global impact; assess reflections.
Inclusivity: Include diverse perspectives; translate resources.

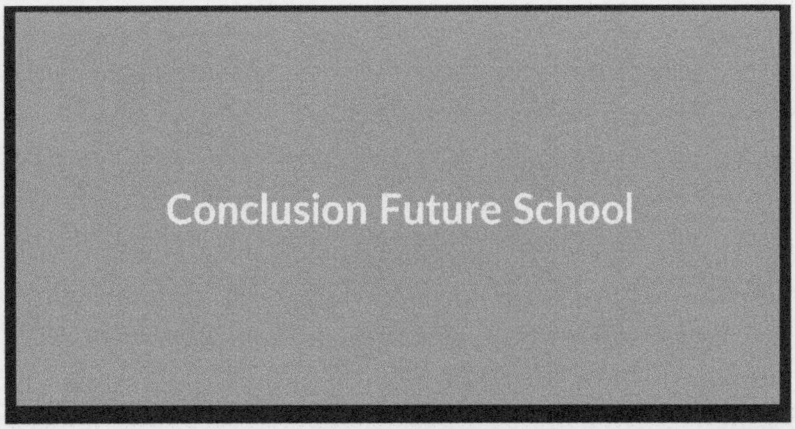

Conclusion: A Call to Build the Global Future School Consortium Together

As the sun rises on June 3, 2025, a new dawn beckons for global education—a chance to weave a future where every child, from bustling cities to quiet villages, learns with joy, grows with purpose, and thrives with equity. The 30 chapters of "The Future School" have painted a vibrant tapestry of possibility: classrooms without walls, curricula that sing with diversity, and teachers who spark dreams. Now, we stand at a crossroads. Nations, governments, educationists, and policymakers, the time to act is now. Let us unite to create the Global Future School Consortium (GFSC), a dynamic movement where every idea, every resource, is shared generously to transform education into the force humanity deserves.

The Vision Realized: Schools as Hubs of Hope

Imagine a world where schools are hubs of hope—where a rural student codes alongside urban peers, where trauma heals through empathy, and where play ignites creativity. These aren't dreams; they're plans laid out in this book. From flexible learning spaces to ethical AI, from restorative practices to career readiness, each chapter offers practical, inclusive strategies, powered by free tools and global collaboration. The GFSC is our vehicle—a consortium where schools in Kenya swap sustainability lessons with those in Brazil, where teachers in India share open-source platforms with colleagues in Canada. Together, we can scale these ideas, ensuring no learner is left behind, no matter their language, ability, or circumstance.

Actionable Calls to Transform

- **Governments:** Rewrite policies to embrace competency-based learning and flexible assessments. Prioritize funding for shared technology and teacher growth, making equity non-negotiable. Implement national frameworks that support the GFSC charter.
- **Educationists:** Champion multilingual curricula and trauma-informed care. Lead professional development initiatives that empower teachers as facilitators and innovators. Foster interdisciplinary collaboration within your institutions.
- **Policymakers:** Allocate resources to establish and expand GFSC initiatives, ensuring access to free, open-source educational tools. Create incentives for schools to adopt sustainable practices and community engagement models.
- **Communities:** Actively participate in shaping local school visions. Volunteer time, share resources, and advocate for inclusive practices. Support student-led projects that address local and global challenges.

Our Collective Future

Conclusion: Our Collective Future

The GFSC's free resources—toolkits, webinars, multilingual guides—make this possible, even in the most resource-scarce corners. In 2025, with 60% of global schools hungry for innovation, the evidence is clear: inclusive models boost engagement by 20%, close gaps by 15%, and prepare students for a world of challenges and opportunities.

The Promise of a Better World

Let's begin this mission with a vision: a future where education doesn't divide but unites, where every child's potential fuels a thriving planet. Picture classrooms buzzing with STEAM projects, communities rallying as partners, and students debating global issues as empowered citizens. This is the future we deserve—one of connection, creativity, and justice. The GFSC is our shared canvas, inviting every nation, every community, and every individual to craft the future school of innovation—a promise of a better world. Join us.

Glossary

Key Terms for The Future School

This glossary provides definitions for key terms and concepts discussed throughout "TheFuture School" booklet. These terms are foundational to understanding the vision for global educational transformation championed by the Global Future School Consortium (GFSC).

Adaptive Learning Platforms
Dynamically adjust content difficulty to match each student's performance, ensuring they are neither overwhelmed nor bored. Examples includeKhan Academy, offering tailored learning paths in subjects like math or reading.

AI Analytics
Provide teachers with actionable insights into student performance by analyzing data from assignments, quizzes, or platform interactions to highlight strengths and areas for improvement. Used to inform instructional decisions and personalise learning efficiently.

AI-DrivenTutoring Systems
Provide instant, personalised support for students, offering real-time guidance on homework or challenging concepts. Tools like Duolingoor Socratic use AI to deliver step-by-step explanations, interactive exercises, or hints tailored to a student's needs, available24/7.

Alumni Networks
Connect current students with graduates who serve as mentors, sharing expertise, career advice, or learning resources to support lifelong education. These networks foster a sense of community and provide role models.

Automated Grading
Systems that use AI to evaluate objective assessments, such as multiple-choice tests or math problems, instantly scoring responses and providing feedback. This automation saves teachers hours, allowing them to focus on creative instruction.

BalancedScreen Time

Ensures technology enhances learning without overshadowing interpersonal interaction, physical engagement, or creative exploration. This involves capping screen-based activities with hands-on activities, group discussions, or outdoor learning.

Block Scheduling
A flexible scheduling model that incorporates longer blocks for deep, project-based work, shorter sessions for targeted skill instruction, and dedicated time for independent study, collaborative activities, and wellness breaks.

Coding Positioned as a foundational skill, enabling students to create digital solutions like apps, games, or websites, fostering creativity and problem-solving. Platforms likeCode.org offer free, beginner-friendly courses.

Collaborative Learning

An approach that prioritises peer-to-peer education, where students work together, share knowledge, and support each other's growth through group projects, peer tutoring, and online collaboration tools.

Community Engagement Transforms schools into vibrant civic and cultural hubs that actively engage with, contribute to, and draw strength from their local and global communities. This includes community service, partnerships with local businesses, and public events. **Community Service**

Integrated into curricula, connecting academic learning with real-world impact through projects like tutoring younger peers or organising park cleanups, fostering civic responsibility and empathy.

Competency-Based Education (CBE)

Redefines success by replacing rigid grade levels with flexible milestones, focusing on mastery of skills (critical thinking, collaboration, creativity) rather than rote memorisation.

Cross-Disciplinary TeacherCollaboration Involves educators from different subjects working together to design integrated lessons, ensuring thematic units are cohesive and impactful, enhancing curriculum coherence and professional growth. **Culturally Responsive Teaching (CRT)** Tailors instruction to honour students' cultural backgrounds, languages, and experiences, making learning relevant and affirming. It fosters engagement by validating identities and building pride.

Curricula Focused onEnvironmentalJustice and Climate Solutions Equip students to address ecological inequities and innovate for a sustainable future, covering topics like renewable energy, carbon sequestration, or policy advocacy. **Curricula Focused onGlobalIssues** Embedding issues like climate change, human rights, or gender equality into curricula makes education relevant and action-oriented, encouraging students to analyse and address real-world challenges.

Cybersecurity Basics

Education that teaches students to protect their digital identities through practices like strong passwords, secure privacy settings, and phishing awareness, fostering safe online behavior.

Digital Literacy The capacity to navigate the complex digital landscape critically, ethically, and confidently, encompassing skills to find, evaluate, create, and communicate information effectively and responsibly online.

Energy-Efficient Facilities
School buildings designed with systems like solar panels or rainwater harvesting, serving as dynamic learning tools to demonstrate renewable energy and conservation in action.

Entrepreneurial Mindsets Cultivating creativity, problem-solving, resilience, resourcefulness, and a proactive approach to identifying and acting on opportunities, preparing students to be architects of their own futures.

Environmental Stewardship
Positioning schools as vibrant hubs for sustainability, embedding principles of environmental responsibility into every facet of their operations, curriculum, and community engagement.

Equity Audits
Transparent policies that create accountability by identifying and addressing biases in school practices, such as discipline, grading, or curriculum content, ensuring fairness for all students. **Ethical AI Integration** A balanced and thoughtful approach to integrating Artificial Intelligence in education, emphasizing its role as a powerful tool to enhance learning while mitigating risks and ensuring human values. **Ethical Discussions about Technology's Societal Impact** Incorporating debates about issues like social media privacy, algorithmic bias, or digital addiction, fostering responsible digital citizenship and critical evaluation of technology.

Flexible Pathways
Allow students to progress at their own pace, accessing advanced content when ready or remedial support when needed, without being locked into a rigid curriculum, using digital platforms, project-based options, and teacher guidance.

Flexible Scheduling Reimagining the school day and year to accommodate diverse learning needs, optimise student engagement, and enhance educational outcomes, moving away from rigid timetables.

FlippedClassroom Model A student-centred method where students watch videos at home to learn content and engage in hands-on activities and discussions in class, with teachers acting as
facilitators.

Global Citizenship
Fostering global understanding, empathy, and informed global citizens who collaborate across borders to address shared challenges, through virtual exchanges and global issue discussions.

GlobalFuture School Consortium (GFSC) A world wide network that unites educators, students, parents, and leaders in a shared mission to make education equitable, innovative, and accessible through open-source resources and collaborative policies.

GlobalIssue Discussions
Connecting students world wide via video conferencing to debate and explore topics like climate change, peace, or inequality, fostering critical thinking and global awareness.

GlobalLearning Networks
Initiatives designed to systematically connect classrooms and students from different countries and cultural backgrounds, fostering cross-cultural dialogue and collaborative problem-solving. **Growth Mindset** The belief that abilities can improve through effort and learning, encouraging students to embrace challenges, persist through setbacks, and view failures as opportunities,
fostering resilience and a love for learning.

Group Projects with DefinedRoles Collaborative projects where students take on specific responsibilities (e.g., leader, scribe, researcher, presenter), teaching accountability, teamwork, and organisational skills.

Independent Learning
Equipping students with the skills to navigate and utilise online resources effectively, fostering self-directed education through platforms like Coursera, edX, or Khan Academy.

Interdisciplinary Learning
A pedagogical approach that breaks down subject silos to reflect the true complexity of the world, weaving together concepts, methods, and perspectives from different fields to foster deeper understanding.

Joint Projects with InternationalSchools
Enable students to collaborate on shared goals, such as creating digital magazine or a sustainability campaign, blending diverse perspectives and skills with peers in other countries.

Language Learning Emphasising Cultural Context Goes beyond grammar, focusing on cultural context to foster appreciation for diverse traditions and perspectives, building intercultural competence and respectful communication.

Lifelong Learning

Equipping students with the skills, mindset, and networks to pursue continuous growth beyond the classroom, adapting to a rapidly changing world.

Maker Spaces

Dedicated areas equipped with tools like3D printers, craft supplies, and recycled materials, where students engage in hands-on STEAM exploration, building prototypes or artworks.

Media Literacy

Lessons on spotting misinformation and bias in media, equipping students to critically evaluate digital content and distinguish credible information from false or biased sources.

MentalHealth Support

Comprehensive integration of mental health resources and supportive practices within educational systems, including on-site counsellors, safe spaces, and stress management education.

Mentorship fromLocalEntrepreneurs

Provides students with real-world insights, inspiration, and guidance, fostering entrepreneurial ambition and resilience through connections with local business owners and innovators.

Mindfulness Exercises

Daily activities such as deep breathing or guided meditations that help students manage stress, reduce anxiety, and sharpen focus, creating a calm foundation for learning.

Modular Classrooms

Equipped with movable furniture like wheeled tables and stackable chairs, transforming spaces into versatile environments that adapt to various activities—group projects, solo study, or class presentations.

Online CollaborationTools

Tools likeGoogle Docs or MicrosoftTeams that enable students to work together in real-time, whether in class or remotely, mimicking modern workplaces and fostering digital fluency.

Open-Source Tools

Software and resources (e.g., Moodle, OpenEd)that are freely available, reducing EdTech costs and making technology accessible to resource-constrained schools while maintaining quality.

Outdoor Learning Areas Spaces that connect students with nature, fostering environmental awareness and well- being through lessons in fresh air, such as science experiments in school gardens or literature discussions under trees.

Parent Advisory Council
A group of parents who provide feedback on school policies, ensuring community voices shape decisions like curriculum choices, extracurricular programs, or safety protocols.

Parent Workshops
Equip families with tools to support learning at home, covering topics like digital literacy, social-emotional learning, or homework strategies, empowering parents to reinforce academic and emotional growth.

Peer Tutoring Programs
Pair older or more advanced students with younger or struggling peers, reinforcing learning for both tutor and tutee, fostering communication and empathy.

Performance-Based Tasks
Assess practical skills like communication, problem-solving, and innovation through activities such as presentations, prototypes, or simulations, reflecting real-world applications.

Personalised Learning
A dynamic, inclusive approach where lessons are tailored to each individual student's unique strengths, interests, and challenges, often powered by adaptive platforms and student-led goals.

Play-Based Learning
Using games and joyful activities to teach concepts, fostering creativity and engagement in an inclusive, cost-effective manner.

ProfessionalAutonomy forTeachers
Grants teachers the freedom to design creative, student-centred lessons without rigid mandates, encouraging innovation tailored to their classrooms' needs.

Project-BasedLearning (PBL)
A pedagogical approach that places real-world problem-solving at its core, transforming classrooms into dynamic spaces where students tackle challenges through collaborative, interdisciplinary projects.

Public Showcases
Events (e.g., fairs, presentations) that allow students to share their project-based learning solutions with authentic audiences—parents, community members, or global peers—making learning meaningful and accountable.

Real-Time Feedback Systems Apps or teacher check-ins that provide instant insights during lessons, enabling
students to improve immediately rather than waiting for graded tests, enhancing learning agility and confidence.

Restorative Practices

Approaches (e.g., restorative circles)that prioritise accountability and community over punitive discipline, building positive, inclusive school cultures. **Safe Spaces** Quiet, welcoming environments within schools (e.g., "calm rooms") for students to process stress or trauma, equipped with comfortable seating, calming visuals, and mindfulness resources.

School Gardens and Composting Programs

Provide hands-on opportunities for students to learn sustainable practices, connecting them directly to ecological systems and demonstrating waste reduction.

Social-EmotionalLearning (SEL) Focuses on embedding SEL into the curriculum to develop emotional intelligence, self-awareness, and interpersonal skills through activities like mindfulness, fostering

empathy and supportive relationships.

Student-Led Goal-Setting

Empowering students to set their own learning goals, aligning education with their passions, fostering intrinsic motivation and ownership, and promoting emotional well-being.

Student-Led"Start-Up" Projects

Empower students to identify and address local challenges by designing innovative solutions, mimicking entrepreneurial processes and developing skills in ideation, budgeting, and marketing.

Student-Driven Questions

Allowing students to propose interdisciplinary research questions, empowering them to guide their learning and fostering curiosity and ownership.

Support Systems for Students with Disabilities or Economic Challenges

Ensure equal access to education through tailored accommodations (e.g., assistive technologies, IEPs) and resources (e.g., devices, internet, supplies) to bridge divides.

Thematic Units

Weave together subjects like history, science, and literature around a central topic (e.g., climate change) to provide a cohesive, real-world learning experience, breaking down subject silos.

Transparent Communication Via digital apps(e.g., ClassDojo) or printed newsletters, keeping parents informed about student progress, school events, and educational goals, fostering trust and collaboration.

Transparent Policies

Address bias and ensure fairness by identifying and addressing biases in school practices (discipline, grading, curriculum), fostering trust and equity for all students.

VirtualExchange Programs

Connect students with peers in other countries through digital platforms (e.g., PenPal Schools), enabling collaborative projects, cultural exchanges, and discussions on shared interests or global issues. **VirtualReality (VR) and AugmentedReality (AR) Spaces** Technologies that create immersive learning environments, transporting students beyond the classroom for experiences like virtual field trips or interactive simulations.

Workshops on Financial Literacy and Innovation

Teach students essential skills like budgeting, investing, and creative problem-solving, preparing them for entrepreneurial and personal success.

Year-Round Schooling

Replaces the traditional long summer break with a balanced calendar (e.g., 9-week terms followed by3-week breaks), minimizinglearning lossandmaintaining academic momentum.

9 789334 355352

Printed at Repro India Ltd.